Testing Spoken English Achievement for Non-English Majors in China

大学英语口语成就测试研究

LI Huadong
李华东

T0114457

Trafford Publishing

Order this book online at www.trafford.com
or email orders@trafford.com

Most Trafford titles are also available at major online book retailers.

Printed in Victoria, BC, Canada.

ISBN: 978-1-4251-5141-6 (sc)

*Our mission is to efficiently provide the world's finest, most comprehensive book publishing
service, enabling every author to experience success. To find out how to publish your book, your
way, and have it available worldwide, visit us online at www.trafford.com*

Trafford rev. 2/16/2010

www.trafford.com

North America & international
toll-free: 1 888 232 4444 (USA & Canada)
phone: 250 383 6864 ◆ fax: 812 355 4082

Contents

Preface

The Spoken English achievement test (SEAT) to be discussed in this book does not refer to the spoken English test as part of the College English Test (CET-SET) held nationwide by the National College English Test Committee for the non-English majors in China. It refers to the spoken English test held by a certain university for the students in that university as part of the end-term or mid-term English examination. It is designed to test the achievement of spoken English as well as to improve (or to exert positive impact on) the teaching and learning of spoken English, hence the name of "the spoken English achievement test".

The SEAT has long been a neglected practice in the achievement test of college English in China. This is partly due to the assumption that such a test is not practical. However, lacking a test of speaking, the end-term or mid-term English achievement test is not able to reflect the learners' overall language proficiency. To make matters worse, this has degraded the teaching and learning of speaking, affected the improvement of overall language proficiency, and thus has failed to meet the needs of society and learners for the speaking skill.

To solve this problem, this book first reviews theories and techniques relevant to speaking and SET, then conducts empirical research into four SEAT formats, and finally puts forward an SEAT format, namely presentation and discussion (P&D).

In theoretical study (part one), a new model of cross-cultural communicative competence for language testing is established, in which both communicative competence (linguistic, pragmatic and strategic) and cross-cultural competence (sensibility, tolerance and flexibility) are encompassed. The literature review also indicates that a direct, criteria-referenced test type is preferable to an indirect, norm-referenced one for the construction of an SEAT, that linguistic input of cross-cultural topics is favorably supplied to candidates, and that the analytical rating method is better than the holistic method in terms of reliability and for the analytical purpose.

In phase one study of the empirical research (part two), four SEAT formats are compared. Empirical evidence confirms the findings in the literature review. It also suggests that the inter-rater reliability of the SEAT is high enough to allow the one-assessor model to be adopted in an SEAT, that content is a necessary assessment criterion, that mini-speech, which mainly resembles the oral presentation technique, is more favorable than role-play and machine-mediated test for an SEAT.

In phase two study of the empirical research (part two), a cross-cultural candidate-centered thematic approach to the SEAT is presented, which favors the cross-cultural topics and situations, encourages interaction among candidates, and requires test tasks in one test to be centered on one broad theme. Afterwards, an SEAT format, namely, the presentation and discussion (P&D), is constructed according to this approach. It is administered in a class of sophomores in Zhejiang University. Statistical analysis shows that this format meets the requirements of validity, reliability and practicality, thus is a "useful" test.

This book is based on "A study of a large-scale spoken English achievement test for non-English majors", a dissertation I submitted in April of 2001 to the Graduate School and the College of Foreign Languages of Zhejiang University in partial fulfillment of the requirements for the MA degree in Linguistics and Applied Linguistics. However, prior to its publication, I have updated this piece of work by adding in new insights and findings from the publications ever since.

This book is a paradoxical creation on two dimensions.

On the time dimension, this book is both "out-dated" and "up-to-date". It is an out-dated product because its publication has been postponed, for this reason and that, by nine years. A few universities have incorporated an SEAT into its mid-term or end-term English examinations since then. However, as a researcher and practitioner of college English teaching, I find that the problem of ignorance of the SEAT is still prevalent in mainland China. I guess this is because this type of test is still considered "impractical", perhaps even more so because of the quick expansion of the population of university students in the recent ten years since China started its program of expanding the recruitment of university students in 1999. This situation has urged me to publish my dissertation because it is intended to solve the problem of "impracticality" of such a test. In the sense that it can help solve an existing problem, this book is still very up-to-date.

On the content dimension, this book is both "practical" and "theoretical". It is practical not only because it is supposed to address a "practical" problem, but it has collected a lot of empirical evidence from the repeated practices of conducting the SEAT. On the other hand, it is theoretical because it has drawn a lot from the theories of speaking and of language testing.

I sincerely hope that this paradoxical book can serve to solve the problem of "impracticality" of the SEAT and promote the practice of and research into such a test in China.

Acknowledgements

I feel grateful to many people, without whom this book would have been impossible. To be specific, the following people are to be credited for their help:

Prof. ZHOU Xing (周星) initializes this book by applying for a research project on a spoken English achievement test in Zhejiang University and later assigning part of this project to the author. During the process of this research, Prof. ZHOU has given insightful advice as well as encouragement and patience to the author.

In phase one study of this book, Prof. SHAO Yongzhen (邵永真) has given me valuable advice. Several classmates of mine, namely, Ms. CHEN Ying (陈颖), Mr. WANG Yi'an (王 安) and Mr. LI Guangcai (李广才), have coordinated with me in a research project on four SEAT formats. This project is done for the writing of term papers of a course entitled Language Testing taught by Prof. SHAO Yongzhen as part of the requirements of the program for MA in Linguistics and Applied Linguistics in Zhejiang University. Moreover, these classmates have been so kind as to allow me to use their data in this book.

In phase two study of this book, some teachers in Zhejiang University have helped with the administration of the Presentation and Discussion (P&D) SEAT to their students. These teachers include Prof. PANG Jixian (庞继贤), Prof. MA Yirong (马以容), Ms. SHOU Sichen (寿似琛) and Ms. JIANG Qian (姜倩). Many students have been willing to be candidates of the tests and to answer the questionnaires in this research. They are sophomores of grade 98 majoring in Computer Software Development in Hangzhou Institute of Electronic Engineering and a band-4 class taught by Prof. MA Yirong in Zhejiang University.

Prior to the publication of the book, Ms. WU Honglan (吴洪兰) helped me in updating relevant literature. Trafford Publishing has given me consistent support and advice during the long time of preparation and editing of the book.

I feel particularly obligated to acknowledge my wife, Ms. SUN Yanjun (孙燕军). She has given me all kinds of support a wife could be able to offer her husband. During the my three-year study in Zhejiang University, she has been kept home 500 kilometers away, maintaining all the house chores, doing her job, taking care of her parents, meanwhile giving birth to and nursing our spectacular daughter, Ms. LI Yunqi (李蕴祺).

Abbreviations

CECR	College English Curriculum Requirements
CET	College English Test
CET-SET	Spoken English Test as a supplement to College English Test
CPE	Certificate of Proficiency in English
CUEFL	Communicative Use of English as a Foreign Language
HKEA-SET	Spoken English Test held by Hong Kong Examinations Authority
IELTS	International English Language Testing System
P&D	presentation and discussion
SEAT	spoken English achievement test
SET	spoken English test
TEM	Test for English Majors
TEM-SET	Spoken English Test as a supplement to Test for English Majors in mainland China
TLU	target language use
TOEFL	Test of English as a Foreign Language
TOEFL-TSE	Test of Spoken English as an optional supplement to Test of English as a Foreign Language
TSE	Educational Testing Service
TT/S	teacher time per student
WTO	World Trade Organization
YU-SET	Spoken English Test in Yarmouk University in Jordan

Chapter 1 Introduction

In this book, I will try to solve a "practical" problem, that is, the general lack of the spoken English achievement test (SEAT) in college English teaching[1] for non-English majors in mainland China. The word "practical" has two denotations here. On the one hand, I will not plan to make theoretical breakthroughs. Rather, I will try to fulfill a keen need for inclusion of a spoken English test in the end-term achievement test of English for non-English majors. In other words, even if some theoretical contributions might be made, they are not my focus. On the other hand, I will pay attention on the "practicality" of such a test, which is widely assumed to be the major obstacle to the application of a large-scale SEAT.

I will begin this book with a brief needs analysis for an SEAT by drawing on my long-term experience as a college English teacher and on wide consultation to relevant people such as teachers, administrators, students as well as employers who come to universities to recruit employees.

1.1 Social needs

After a study of the history of objective testing, especially that of TOEFL, Spolsky (1995) found that it is usually the economic and social factors rather than breakthroughs in testing theories and techniques that underline the development of testing. Therefore, according to Spolsky, testing developers should "divert attention to some of the external,

---

[1] The term of "college English" is generally used to refer to English teaching to non-English majors in colleges and universities in mainland China. This is usually conducted by a course bearing this name. This course is mainly designed for freshmen and sophomores, although some advanced courses combining English teaching and their specialties (therefore can be described as English for Specific Purposes) are also taught in a few universities. The Spoken English achievement test (SEAT) to be discussed in this book does not refer to the spoken English test as part of the College English Test (CET-SET) held nationwide by the National College English Test Committee for the non-English majors in China. It refers to the spoken English test held by a certain university for the students in that university as part of the end-term or mid-term English examination. It is designed to test the achievement of spoken English as well as to improve (or to exert positive impact on) the teaching and learning of spoken English, hence the name of "the spoken English achievement test".

non-theoretical, institutional, social forces that, on deeper analysis, often turn out to be much more powerful explanations of actual language teaching practice." (Spolsky, 1995: 2)

Is there a social need for an SEAT in Chinese colleges and universities? Most people would say "yes". After China joined the World Trade Organization (WTO) and later became a "world factory", Chinese policies are becoming more and more "open" to the outside world. This increasing "openness" means more and more face-to-face interaction between Chinese and foreigners. Even ordinary people may realize that they encounter foreigners much more frequently than before in the streets of Chinese cities and towns. Whatever they do, Chinese college graduates may need to talk with foreigners. And they tend to do so mainly in English, because it has become an established world language.

This trend is reflected in the job-hunting of college students. In the past, most employers would require a pass certificate of the college English test (CET) held nationwide in China. But in recent years, quite a few companies require job applicants to be able to speak English. Some of the job interviewers from recognized international corporations are even foreigners. As one of the employers claim, "we do not want a person who is merely able to show us his certificates. What we need are those who are able to display the ability to communicate efficiently with our foreign clients in spoken English." This is not rare remark people hear at a job interview in recent years.

Although there is already a spoken English test (CET-SET) held by the committee of college English testing, there is a need for an SEAT in Chinese universities. For one thing, without an SEAT, learners are not able to evaluate their progress during their study. As is well known, the CET-SET is only held when learners finish their required English courses. But during their study of the courses, they have no way of assessing their spoken English. For another, CET-SET is only available to a minority of top students, because CET-SET requires its test takers to have a very high score in the written test of CET before it provides such an opportunity for them. For this reason, the desire of the other students for a spoken English test (SET) is neglected. This is not only unfair, but also impractical, because there might be students who is not that good at written English tests but might be able to speak English fairly well. To test this hypothesis, I tried an experiment in which two native speakers of English took a standard written test of CET. To our surprise, one of them scored lower than the required mark for a CET-SET, which means that he might not be allowed

2

to take part in CET-SET if he were a Chinese non-English major.

1.2 Learners' needs

Students usually hate tests because there are already too many of them. But do they hate an SEAT too? To find out the answer, I asked a

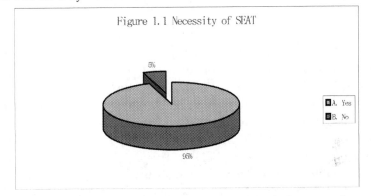

group of students (110 subjects) whether they believe such a test is necessary in one questionnaire survey of this book (see Appendix 11). To our surprise, the vast majority of them (95%) believe that it is necessary to have an SEAT at the end of each term (see figure 1.1).

I also asked the students why they believe an SEAT is necessary if they do think so. The result of this question is shown in Table 1.1.

Table 1.1 Reasons for the necessity of an SEAT

Reasons	Number	Percentage
1) Speaking is an important skill.	31	82%
2)The SEAT can promote oral practice.	17	45%
3) Speaking should be tested separately because written tests do not necessarily reveals oral competence.	19	50%
4) Speaking is becoming increasingly important with the growing of cross-cultural communication.	29	76%
5) Other reasons	14	37%

From table 1.1, we can see that the majority of the subjects think that an SEAT is necessary because of the importance of speaking as a skill (82%) and as a tool for cross-cultural communication (76%). Half of them believe speaking should be tested separately as an implementation for written tests.

1.3 Problems caused by neglecting the SEAT

Even though there is such a wide and urgent need for an SEAT, it is neglected in practice. In discussion with relevant people, I find that this negligence results in the following negative effects.

1) Without an SEAT, the evaluation of learners' overall English proficiency is inadequate or incomplete. According to previous research (such as 文秋芳, 1999), the correlation between a reliable SET and written tests is roughly around 0.4-0.6. This means that although speaking is correlated to other skills, the correlation is not very high. This means that good performance in the written tests does not guarantee good speaking ability. This is probably one important reason why many influential English tests, such as CUEFL, IELTS, TOEFL, TEM (Test for English Majors) and CET (College English Test), include a test of spoken English.

2) Speaking has long been ignored in the practice of teaching and learning. Any tests, especially those given for a selective purpose, have impact or "backwash effect" on teaching and learning. Because there is not such an SEAT, the skill of speaking has long been ignored in the practice of English teaching and learning. In some classrooms, things even go to the extreme: the teacher dominates the classroom by "lecturing" on knowledge of the English language, while the students are given very little time to practice speaking. This does not include the worst occasions in which in some universities the class hours are occupied by written simulation tests several weeks prior to CET.

3) The employers have no way of getting information of the job applicants' oral English proficiency. Today, more and more companies extend their business to the world. In turn, most of them need to know how well the job applicants communicate with foreigners in oral English. They are usually provided with a list of the courses the applicants take with scores on it. But they are not able to find a score of an SEAT. Of course, it is unlikely for them to arrange an SET by themselves in the job interview because they have neither the obligation nor the qualification to hold such a test.

1.4 Is a large-scale SEAT really "impractical"?

Then why don't the universities, or to be specific, the teachers of English, hold such a test? Most teachers and administrators would assume that a large-scale SEAT is impractical. But is this true? In other words, do they give this assumption on the basis of research or on groundless speculations? Are there any research projects that imply such a test is practical at all?

I did not find any research that defines a large-scale SET as impractical. On the contrary, I do find one that claims to have held a large-scale oral test to around 2000 candidates within the limitations of practicality (Walker, 1990). This further encourages my attempt to find a practical way of conducting the SEAT in the situation of Chinese college English teaching.

1.5 Organization of this book

This book is roughly divided into two parts.

Part one is a literature review of theories and practice relevant tothe SEAT. In this part, chapter two deals with theories of speaking, chapter three discusses theories of testing, and chapter four compares several influential SET formats. In this part, the implications of these theories and practice on the SEAT design are also included.

Part two is empirical studies on the SEAT formats. As the phase one study, chapter five illustrates several SEAT formats held by me and co-researchers in Zhejiang University. In the phase two study, chapter six presents the detailed procedure of an SEAT format designed by the researcher, namely the presentation and discussion (P&D) format, and chapter seven gives an evaluation of this format based on statistical analysis.

In the end, chapter eight concludes the findings of this book and discusses implications for further research.

Part one: Theoretical studies

Part one includes three chapters, namely chapter 2, chapter 3 and chapter 4. Chapter 2 tries to review theories of speaking with an attempt to answer the question of "what" the SEAT is supposed to measure. Chapter 3 attempts to revisit theories of language testing so as to answer the question of "how" the SEAT is going to measure what it is supposed to measure. Chapter 4 will compare and contrast some of the most influential spoken English tests so as to get useful hints for our SEAT design.

Chapter 2 Theories of speaking and their implications for the SEAT design

Before a test is designed, it is necessary to consider "what" the test is supposed to measure. Of course, a spoken English test is intended to measure the English "speaking" ability. But what constitutes "speaking" ability? What implications does it have for a SAET design? These two seemingly self-evident questions still deserve the test designers' attention because the available different test formats clearly indicate that different test designers have different beliefs on the simple word "speaking". For example, some scholars proposed a multiple-choice written test of speaking. A typical item goes like this:

X: I hope you don't mind my pointing out your mistake.

Y: _____.

    A) Of course

    B) Not at all

    C) You are very welcome

    D) Yes, I don't (Howe, 1983: 182)

This format is apparently aimed at achieving objectivity and efficiency of marking. However, it reveals that the designers of this test format consider speaking more as knowledge than as a skill. Moreover, it has the danger of sacrificing the content validity. One might ask: can a test of speaking be conducted in written form? Of course, a written test does measure candidates' grammar and vocabulary. If designed properly, it could measure pronunciation. But to what degree can it measure pragmatic competence? Is it able to evaluate fluency and strategic competence?

In this chapter, a brief literature review will be done to explore the theories of speaking and to discuss their implications for the SEAT design. It seeks to answer the following six questions:

1) What is speaking? Is it a skill or a type of knowledge?

2) What constitute the so-called "communicative competence"?

3) Is speaking of English as a foreign language cross-cultural in nature?

4) What kinds of "input" or "stimuli" are appropriate for a test of speaking?

5) What does the "student-centered thematic approach" of teaching mean to a test of spoken English?

6) What are the requirements of speaking in College English Syllabus?

2.1 Speaking: a skill or knowledge?

The distinction between knowledge and skill is crucial in the teaching and testing of speaking. Different understandings of speaking will certainly result in different test designs, as is shown in the above example. But is speaking basically knowledge or a skill?

It is obvious that in order to be able to speak a foreign language, it is necessary for one to know some knowledge of grammar and vocabulary. But speaking is more than just *knowing* how to assemble sentences in the abstract sense. A speaker has to produce them and adapt them to the circumstances. This means making decisions rapidly, implementing them smoothly, and adjusting his conversation as unexpected problems appear in communication.

The distinction between language knowledge and skills could be traced to early 1960s. Lado (1961) believed that foreign language proficiency could be classified into skills (listening, speaking, reading and writing) and knowledge (grammar, vocabulary, and phonology/graphology). Bachman (1990) identified two defects in Lido's framework. One is that it did not indicate how skills and knowledge are related. The other is that it failed to recognize the full context of language use – the context of discourse and situation.

Bygate (1987) also attempted to distinguish between language knowledge and language skill. He described the former as "basically a set of grammar and pronunciation rules, vocabulary, and knowledge about how they are normally used", while the latter as "the ability to use them". Then, he tried to analyze the relationship between them, which is shown in figure 2.1.

In Bygate's view, speaking incorporates the following kinds of skills:

Firstly, it is the ability to manipulate grammar and vocabulary, and pronounce it correctly. Beyond this, however, oral language is not just written language spoken. Speech involves the use of production skills, notably facilitation[2] and compensation devices[3]. It also involves the skill of resolving specific kinds of communication problems. These are firstly the negotiation of meaning (explicitness[4] and procedures[5]), and secondly the management of interaction (turn-taking[6] and agenda management[7]). (Bygate, 1987: 49)

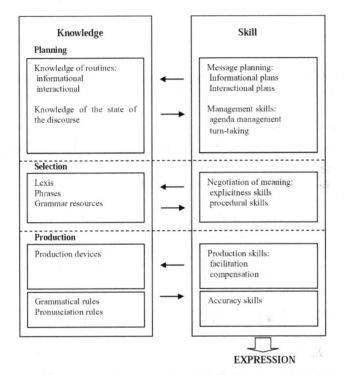

Figure 2.1 A summary of oral skills (Bygate, 1987: 50)

But what are the interrelationships between language knowledge and skill? According to Bygate, skills are dependent on some appropriate knowledge resource, and knowledge is accumulated, on the other hand, through skill use, "as negotiation routines are invented and repeated and refined by the user, they are likely to be stored in the memory as the

---

[2] facilitation: devices for enabling the speaker to be more efficient in his or her production of language

[3] compensation devices/strategies: ways of communicating by improvising temporary substitutes when the speaker lacks normal language

[4] explicitness: degree to which information is stated rather than assumed

[5] procedures: ways of transposing meaning into words and checking understanding

[6] turn-taking: the process of exchanging the role of speaker in a conversation

[7] agenda management: deciding what topic to speak on at what moment, and how to divide topics up

speaker finds them useful or successful." (Bygate, 1987: 49)

Then, what exactly is the difference between knowledge and skill? Bygate points out that "a fundamental difference is that while both can be understood and memorized, only a skill can be imitated and practiced". (Bygate, 1987: 4)

Although Bygate, like Lado, didn't mention the influence of the context of discourse and situation on speaking, his distinction between knowledge and skill and his analysis of the interrelationship between them give us important hints on the designing of spoken English test (SET). One is that if speaking is seen as a skill rather than mere knowledge, it should not be tested the same way as vocabulary, grammar or phonology. The written test format of speaking, as is mentioned in the beginning of this chapter, can only test whether the candidate knows how to use certain aspect of language, but cannot really test the use of that knowledge itself. In other words, speaking can only be tested by actually facilitating the candidates to speak! Moreover, if speaking as a skill is composed of the sub-skills of planning, selection and production, the rating criteria of a successful SET should also include not only accuracy, but also the production skills such as facilitation, compensation, and negotiation of meaning and even planning.

2.2 Revisiting "communicative competence"

As was mentioned in 2.1, Bygate defined the language skill as "the ability to use language knowledge". A closely related term for "ability" is what is often referred to as "competence". From the above analysis, Bygate's definition of language skill can be roughly interpreted as "linguistic competence" often quoted by many scholars, although in his framework, some aspects of strategic competence such as some planning and production skills are also mentioned.

Later studies focused more on "communicative competence" (Hymes, 1972; Canale & Swain, 1980; Canale, 1983; Bachman, 1990; 李筱菊, 1997; 文秋芳, 1999), in which, linguistic competence only accounted for part of it. It would be difficult to market a new large-scale test that did not claim to be 'communicative' – whatever the term might mean for different users (Fulcher, 2000). In this section, a brief comparison will be done among four different models of communicative competence.

2.2.1 Canale & Swain's model

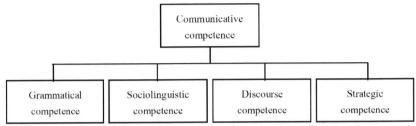

Figure 2.2 Canale & Swain's model of communicative competence

Canale and Swain's model of communicative competence included four components (Canale & Swain, 1980; Canale, 1983; Swain, 1984):

a) grammatical competence, including vocabulary, word formation, sentence formation, pronunciation, spelling and linguistic semantics;

b) sociolinguistic competence, addressing the extent to which utterances are produced and understood appropriately in different sociolinguistic contexts depending on contextual factors such as status of participants, purposes of the interaction, and norms or conventions of interaction;

c) discourse competence, concerning mastery of how to combine grammatical forms and meanings to achieve a unified spoken or written text in different genres;

d) strategic competence, composed of mastery of verbal and non-verbal communication strategies that may be called into action to compensate for breakdowns in communication due to constrictions in actual situations or to insufficient competence in one or more other areas of communicative competence and to enhance the effectiveness of communication.

Canale and Swain's model, although quite popular in 1980s, is problematic in that it did not specify the relationship of the four components (HAN, 2000: 48). Another deficiency of this model is that it did not pay enough attention to cross-cultural factors (文秋芳, 1999: 9). It is assumed that Canale and Swain are more concerned with the non-native speaker in mind than Chomsky or Hymes since they have extended the notion of communicative competence to include the ability of strategic use of language, which non-native speakers are generally supposed to have more problems when they try to use a second or foreign language (XU, 1998: 212). But Canale and Swain did not go further to explore how cross-cultural differences may affect the different components of communicative competence. XU argues that, among the four components in Canale and Swain's model, while grammatical competence and strategic competence can be seen as independent of the culture in which it is acquired, sociolinguistic competence and discourse competence are highly cultural-specific.

2.2.2 Bachman's model

Bachman (1990) proposed a model of communicative language ability (CLA), which is illustrated in figure 2.3.

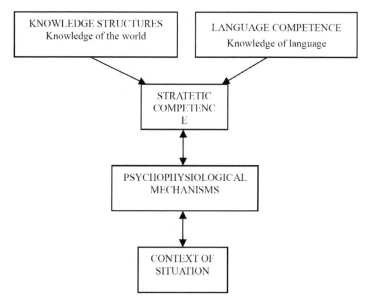

Figure 2.3 Components of communicative language ability in communicative language use (Bachman, 1990: 85)

Bachman further divided language competence into organizational competence (including grammatical competence and textual competence) and pragmatic competence (including illocutionary competence and sociolinguistic competence). He also believed that strategic competence performs such functions as assessment, planning and execution. As knowledge structure and context of situation are not the primary goal of language teaching, and psychophysilogical mechanisms are considered out of scope of our discussion, Bachman's model of communicative language ability can be simplified into figure 2.4.

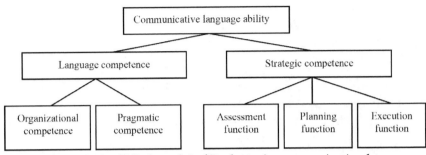

Figure 2.4 A simplified model of Bachman's communicative language ability

Bachman's model is much more complicated than Canale and Swain's and it explains how the components of communicative competence are related to one another, i.e., strategic competence serves as a bridge between language competence and knowledge structure, and then, through psychophysilogical mechanisms, apply knowledge of language and that of the world to the context of situation. It is also different from Canale and Swain's model in that his notion of strategic competence has different denotations. While Canale and Swain's strategic competence refers more to the communicative strategies (mostly compensation), Bachman's is more similar to learning strategies (basically meta-cognitive strategies) (O'Malley & Chamot, 1990; Oxford, 1990; 文秋芳, 1999: 7). Nevertheless, although it takes into account the factor of knowledge of the world, Bachman's model does not emphasize the importance of the cross-cultural knowledge or competence, which is believed critical for non-native speakers of a language (文秋芳, 1999: 7).

2.2.3 李筱菊's model

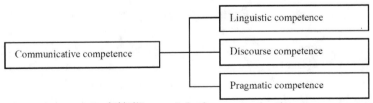

Figure 2.5 李筱菊's model of communicative competence

李筱菊 (1997) put forward her own model of communicative competence on the basis of previous ones. She believed that

13

communicative competence is composed of three subcategories (see figure 2.5). The linguistic competence refers to both language knowledge and language skills. Discourse competence means the use of language beyond sentence level. Pragmatic competence is considered as the ability to use language in real situations.

李筱菊 used a metaphor to illustrate the relationship among the three components of communicative competence: "Communicative competence is a compound rather than a mixture." According to her model, the different components cannot be tested in isolation. Instead, communicative competence should be tested as a whole.

2.2.4 文秋芳's model of cross-cultural communicative competence

Compared with the above three models, 文秋芳's model (文秋芳, 1999) of cross-cultural communicative competence is more useful for testing non-native speakers of English as it added a separate component, namely, cross-cultural competence, to the traditional models of communicative competence (see figure 2.6).

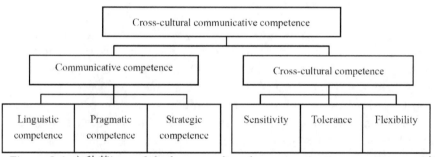

Figure 2.6 文秋芳's model of cross-cultural communicative competence (文秋芳, 1999: 9)

According to 文秋芳, linguistic competence includes both grammatical competence (vocabulary, grammar, phonology) and discourse competence (cohesion and coherence), pragmatic competence includes both functional competence (the ability to understand and perform certain functions in a given situation) and sociolinguistic competence (the sensitivity to, or control of the conventions of language use that are determined by the features of the specific context, for example, sensitivity to differences in dialect or variety and sensitivity to differences in register). The strategic competence in her model has the same content as that in

Canale and Swain's model.

In 文秋芳's cross-cultural competence, sensibility refers to the ability to sense the cross-cultural differences not only at the visible or superficial level such as language, food, clothing, etc., but also at the invisible or deep level such as social belief, value concepts, attitude and communication rules, etc. Tolerance means adopting an attitude of understanding and respect to cultural differences. Flexibility involves two abilities. One is the ability to adjust one's own behavior to different cultural backgrounds of both parties in communication so as to achieve communicative goals. The other is the ability to handle conflicts caused by cultural differences.

Although 文秋芳 regarded strategic competence as an important component of her model of communicative competence, she did not include learning strategy in her description of strategic competence. According to Cohen (1998: 5), learner strategies encompass both language learning and language use strategies (see figure 2.7). If a model of communicative competence is intended to be beneficial for teaching and measurement of a second or foreign language, then there is reason to believe that the exclusion of learning strategies makes the model incomplete. Although some learning strategies, like making plans for language learning, may not contribute directly to communication, they should be encouraged in teaching and testing, especially in achievement or progress tests, for the long-term positive impact on learning.

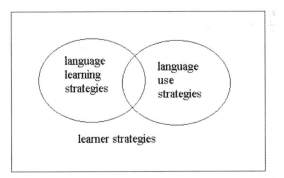

Figure 2. 7 The relationship between language learning strategies and language use strategies

2.2.5 A comparison and contrast of the four models

A brief comparison and contrast of the four models is summarized in table 2.1. Although the four models are different, they all include linguistic competence (within and beyond sentence level, i.e., at both grammatical and discourse levels) and pragmatic competence (which Canale and Swain referred to as sociolinguistic competence).

Table 2.1 a comparison of the four models of communicative competence

Canale & Swain	Bachman	李筱菊	文秋芳
Grammatical competence	Organizational competence	Linguistic competence	Linguistic competence
Discourse competence		Discourse competence	
Sociolinguistic competence	Pragmatic competence	Pragmatic competence	Pragmatic competence
Strategic competence (compensation)	Strategic competence (meta-cognitive strategies)		Strategic competence (compensation and negotiation)
			Cross-cultural competence

However, although strategic competence appeared in three models, it has different definitions. In Canale and Swain's model it mainly pointed to compensation strategies, which occur only when communication breaks down. In Bachman's model, it denoted meta-cognitive strategies such as assessment, planning and execution. In 文秋芳's model, it referred to both compensation and negotiation strategies, the former being used in expression of meaning, and the latter, in acquiring meaning. In this sense, 文秋芳's model is more similar to Canale and Swain's model than to Bachman's model.

文秋芳's model made an important supplement to the former scholars' effort in that it included a cross-cultural competence, which will be of increasing importance for language learners with the rapid development of cross-cultural communication.

A closer look at the four models reveals two major deficiencies in them:

Firstly, a comparison and contrast of the four models with Bygate's model of oral skills would show that knowledge of the world and knowledge of the language and their relationship with competence are not specified in three models of communicative competence. Although Bachman did mention knowledge of the world and knowledge of language, he did not point out which part of knowledge should be focused on in second/foreign language teaching and testing. Some scholars argue that "competence" is more related to skill than to knowledge and that competence is thought of "transferable" while knowledge is not. For example, having the knowledge of the cultural differences between Chinese and Americans only enables Chinese learners of English to overcome cultural barriers when communicating with Americans, but cannot help them to achieve this goal with dealing with, say, Arabians. However, having cross-cultural competence, such as sensitivity, tolerance and flexibility, would enable Chinese learners to communicate with people of any nations (文秋芳，1999:12). However, knowledge, whether conscious or unconscious, is thought of as the basis on which competence is cultivated.

Secondly, in the first three models, cross-cultural competence was neglected. Even in 文秋芳's model, how cross-cultural dimension is tested was not specified.

2.2.6 A tentative model of cross-cultural communicative competence for SET

After a brief review of the major theories on communicative competence (including cross-cultural communicative competence), a tentative model of cross-cultural communicative competence is put forward here (see figure 2.8).

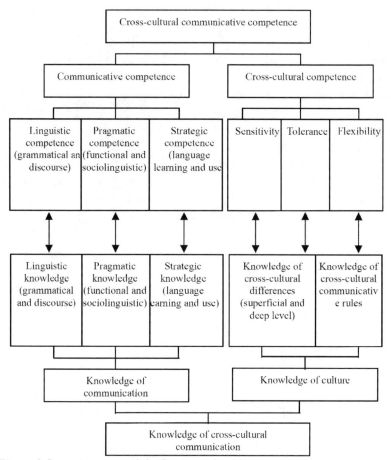

Figure 2.8 a tentative model of cross-cultural communicative competence
constructed for second/foreign teaching and testing

This model makes two modifications to the existing ones based upon the discussion above.

Firstly, it demonstrates the relationship between knowledge and competence/skill. Although it is competence that second/foreign language teaching is intended to develop and that second/foreign language testing is supposed to measure, a model of competence is incomplete without referring to its relationship with knowledge. It is true that the communicative approach does not stop at making learners merely "know" about the language. It may not even teach language knowledge in an explicit way. But whether it is conscious learning of knowledge in some cases, or it is subconscious "acquiring" of it in some others, there is no denying that competence is dependent upon knowledge. Conversely, during the growth of competence, knowledge is accumulated.

This modification may have positive implications for second/foreign language teaching and testing. While keeping the cultivation of competence in mind, the knowledge aspect should not be devaluated. On the one hand, the teacher/examiner should not feel guilty if they arrange their lessons/tests to directly or indirectly teach/assess the use of language knowledge. One the other hand, in order to improve the so-called cross-cultural competence, the contents of teaching/testing should preferably be focused upon cross-cultural topics.

Secondly, strategic competence includes strategies for both language learning and language use in the new model. If a model of competence is constructed for the teaching and testing of the target language, the learning strategies cannot be left out. Even though some learning strategies do not contribute directly to communication, they should be included for the benefit of teaching and learning. For example, some language learners repeatedly refer to a handy dictionary, or to other people, for the meaning or pronunciation of an unfamiliar word during oral communication. Although this practice may be boring and even interfering with communication, it should be encouraged because it may be helpful for language learning.

How, to be specific, can strategic competence be tested in second/foreign language testing? To answer this question, a brief literature review must be made of studies into test-taking strategies. Second/foreign language learner strategies encompass both second/foreign language learning and second/foreign language use strategies. Language learning strategies can be further classified into direct (including memory strategies, cognitive strategies and compensation strategies) and indirect strategies (including metacognitive strategies, affective strategies and social strategies) (Oxford, 1990: 16), or into metacognitive, cognitive and social/affective (O'Malley & Chamot, 1990: 46). Second/foreign language use strategies are also categorized into four subsets: retrieval strategies, rehearsal strategies, cover strategies and communication strategies (Cohen, 1998: 5-7).

Although the process of test taking is usually regarded as pseudo-communication, strategies in coping with a language test can also encompass language learning strategies and language use strategies. These grouped together are called "contributory strategies" in the present study because they do, to some degree, contribute to language learning and/or language use.

Besides these strategies, candidates are also apt to take some "test-wiseness strategies", which are not necessarily determined by proficiency in the language being assessed, but rather may be dependent on the respondent's knowledge of how to take tests (Cohen, 1998: 219). Cohen notes that these "test-wiseness strategies" may be a misnomer, since they are sometimes not so wise. For example, in a study of test-taking strategies in Israel, one college student respondent was seen to produce a written translation of an entire Hebrew foreign language text before he was willing to respond to questions dealing with that text. For this reason, and also for the reason that these strategies are not contributory to language learning and use, these "test-wiseness strategies" are termed "noncontributory strategies" in this book. Thus, test-taking strategies can be classified in figure 2.9.

Figure 2.9 Classification of strategies employed by candidates in SET

Based on the above considerations, it is argued here that if an SET takes strategic competence into account, it should encourage the contributory strategies rather than the noncontributory ones. Thus, in rating candidates, the assessor should merit the use of contributory strategies, and demerit the noncontributory ones. Conversely, to judge whether a test is good or not, one should also think about whether this test encourages the use of contributory strategies while discourages the use of noncontributory ones.

2.3 Features of spoken language

Speaking, as a skill, is different from other skills, even from writing, which is also a productive skill. According to Bygate (1987: 7-9), there are at least two factors that can affect the nature of speech. The first is termed "processing conditions", which refers to the fact that speech takes place under the pressure of time. The other is called "reciprocity conditions", which means the direct and, in most cases, face-to-face relationship between the speaker and listener in the process of speech.

The processing conditions of oral language result in certain common language features. They are as follows (Bygate, 1987: 20):

1) *Adjustments*: hesitations, false starts, self-corrections, rephrasing, and circumlocutions;

2) *Syntactic features*: ellipsis and parataxis;

3) *Repetition*: via expansion or reduction;

4) *Formulaic expressions*.

Why do SET designers have to be aware of these features of speech that are different from those of writing? One reason is that the natural speech of native speakers may display these features, thus these features should be reflected in the rating scale. Traditional English teaching in primarily intended to enable learners to orally produce grammatically correct sentences without paying much attention to these normal features of speech. If learners fail to produce complete sentences, they are made to feel discouraged or even ashamed to speak out. This approach to oral instruction is one of the reasons why so many "dumb" English learners have been cultivated. Even though a few learners are able to speak, the majority of them speak very bookish English. This approach to language teaching was also reflected in SET. For example, a Chinese teacher might reduce the score of a candidate if he or she produces "incomplete" sentences. However, considering the fact that ellipsis is one important feature of speaking, this scoring approach sounds unreasonable and unjust. The following kinds of conversation are not uncommon in the language classroom:

What is your name? ... My name is John.

Where do you live? ... I live in Canterbury.

What is your address? ... My address is 19 The Green.

Did you enjoy the cinema the other day? ... No, I didn't enjoy the cinema the other day. The cinema the other day was closed.

Do the answers need to be in full sentences? In most cases, even native speakers may use ellipsis. To them, such answers in complete sentences may sound strange and unnecessary, or they might generate certain unpleasant implied meanings.

The other reason why SET designers have to notice these features of speech is that these features actually help learners to speak, and help them to learn to speak. If an SET is intended to have positive backwash effect on learning, it should allow and even encourage the display of these features in candidates' performance.

2.4 What type of input should be provided in SET: the input and output hypotheses

One important question in designing an SET is whether it is necessary to provide linguistic input to candidates. If it is necessary, then what kind of input is desirable for an SET? A brief review of the influential input hypothesis and output hypothesis may be of help in answering this question.

Krashen (1985: 2-3) claims that humans acquire language in only one way – by understanding messages, or by receiving "comprehensible input". He used a formula "i+1" to describe what he meant by "comprehensible input", where "i" refers to the learner's current level and "1" means unacquired language. According to him, learners are able to understand language containing unacquired grammar (in a broad sense) with the help of context, which includes extra-linguistic information, our knowledge of the world, and previously acquired linguistic competence. The input hypothesis has two corollaries:

- Speaking is basically a result of acquisition but not its cause. Speech cannot be taught directly but "emerges" on its own as a result of building competence via comprehensible input.

- If input is understood, and there is enough of it, the necessary grammar is automatically provided. The language teacher need not attempt deliberately to teach the next structure along the natural order – it will be provided in just the right quantities and automatically reviewed if the student receives a sufficient amount of comprehensible input.

However, Swain (1995) disagrees with Krashen, who degrades the functions of output in language acquisition. She then put forward an "output hypothesis" (Swain, 1995: 125-144), which claims that language production serves second language acquisition in several ways. It not only can enhance fluency, but also can improve accuracy by performing three functions:

- The noticing/triggering function: This function can also be referred to as consciousness-raising function. It means that in producing the target language, learners may encounter a linguistic problem leading them to notice what they do not know, or know only partially. In other words, the activity of producing the target language may prompt second language learners to consciously recognize some of their linguistic problems; it may make them aware of something they need to find out about L2.

- The hypothesis-testing function: This function means that learners may use their output as a way of trying out new language forms and structures as they stretch their interlanguage to meet communicative needs; they may produce output just to see what works and what does not.

- The metalinguistic/reflective function: This function means that learners may use language to reflect on language, which allows them to control and internalize it. The term "metalinguistic" means that in performing this function, the learners use other language forms to talk about the target language.

The two seemingly contradictory hypotheses are actually complementary in nature. In acquiring a second/foreign language, one has to receive adequate "comprehensible input", and meanwhile he has to use the target language to get to know about his progress and problems, to try out new forms and to reflect on his progress.

The complementary nature of the two hypotheses has important implications for both second/foreign language instruction and assessment. On the one hand, the output hypothesis gives output (speaking and writing) its desired weight. This makes the different output-oriented activities in teaching and testing reasonable. On the other hand, the input hypothesis provides an important constraint under which output may be generated, i.e., if we want to get language production, either in teaching or testing, appropriate language input has to be provided.

One might argue that the input under testing circumstances does not have to be linguistic. They could be visual prompts such as pictures and real objects. But no one could deny the fact that even in such cases the instructions of the test have to be linguistic. Of course, in large-scale proficiency tests, such as writing tests in CET band 4 and 6, the instructions or even outlines can be in candidates' mother tongue. It was claimed that this practice is intended to prevent candidates from copying the outlines into their writing (杨惠中 & Weir, 1998: 36). This might be advantageous for a proficiency test, but might undermine the impact of testing on teaching, thus should be avoided in an achievement test, in which the impact is considered significant.

Then what type of input is preferable in an achievement SET? From the above discussion, the optimal input or prompt might be "comprehensible input", mostly linguistic, which resembles that used in the teaching and learning of spoken English. This is to achieve positive impact or backwash effect on teaching. But certainly this should be done within the limit of practicality, which is also one important concern in carrying out an achievement SET. This issue will be discussed in the later chapters.

2.5 Student-centered thematic model: What does it mean to SET?

A student-centered thematic model of English teaching is in practice in Zhejiang University. It is the result of several years of research and practice aiming at reforming college English teaching (应惠兰，何莲珍，周颂波, 1998). Since this has aroused considerable concern in China (e.g. 罗伟, 1999), a brief introduction to this approach and its implications for SET design will be discussed here.

The student-centered thematic approach is theoretically based upon learner-centered approach, the input and output hypothesis and relevant theories on textbook development. It features student-centered reading and listening activities directed by the teacher, cultivation of integrative skills of language by way of arranging all activities around carefully chosen themes, and a new textbook series to embody this approach. After several years of empirical research, this approach has achieved considerable success (应惠兰，何莲珍，周颂波, 1998).

One result of this approach is the publishing of a textbook series for college English teaching, namely 'New College English" (NCE). In NCE, each unit is centered on one theme and is composed of four sections: preparation, listening-centered activities, reading-centered activities, and further development. The preparation section is intended to arouse learners' interest in the theme, to stimulate their thinking on the theme, and to prepare them for the in-depth input of language and content soon to come. The activities centered on listening and reading are intended to provide adequate comprehensible input. Finally, the further development section supplies integrated communicative activities for learners to confirm and use the language they acquired in the listening and reading.

24

In this textbook series, a variety of classroom organizations are included, with group work among the learners being the central form of organization. Meanwhile, presentation and discussion by the learners are highly encouraged.

What does this model mean to our SET design? If an SET is intended to achieve high content validity and positive backwash effect, it should also reveal the approach to teaching. This model of English teaching has at least two implications for SET design. First, in our SET, the candidates should be the center of communication while the examiners should preferably be as invisible as possible except for giving the instructions and ensuring the procedure of testing process. For this reason, the candidate-centered testing formats or techniques such as presentation, discussion, role-play are more favorable than the more tester-centered ones such as interviews (unless the candidate plays the role of the interviewer). Second, the testing activities should preferably resemble those in teaching in that they'd better be centered on one theme. If every candidate is talking about a different topic irrelevant to those of other candidates, it is unlikely to facilitate reciprocal communication. Integrating this belief with the input hypothesis and the model of cross-cultural communicative competence discussed above, sufficient linguistic input centered on a cross-cultural theme should preferably be given to candidates prior to their performance. Of course, this should also be constrained into the practical domain.

2.6 The requirements for speaking in College English Curriculum Requirements (CECR)

The priority to be considered before designing a test is whether it tests what is supposed to be tested. An achievement test is supposed to test what is taught. If we want to design an SEAT, we should have a brief understanding of what is, or supposed to be, taught. Thus, to achieve content validity, we should study the requirements for speaking in College English Curriculum Requirements (CECR) before designing the SEAT.

Among the requirements of spoken English in the new college English teaching syllabus, there are four parts worth discussing.

2.6.1 Objective of college English teaching

The objective of College English is to develop students' ability to use English in an all-round way, especially in listening and speaking, so that in their future work and social interactions they will be able to exchange information effectively through both spoken and written channels, and at the same time they will be able to enhance their ability to study independently and improve their cultural quality so as to meet the needs of China's social development and international exchanges. (教育部高等教育司，2007：1)

In developing competence in listening, speaking, reading, writing and translation at the three levels mentioned above, college and universities should lay more stress on the cultivation and training of listening and speaking abilities. … Moreover, colleges and universities should cover components of learning strategies and intercultural communication in their teaching so as to enhance students' abilities of independent learning and of communication. (教育部高等教育司，2007：5)

There are three points worth mentioning.

1) Speaking is given equal importance to listening. Both speaking and listening are given more importance than writing and translating.

2) The training of spoken English should be oriented toward communication for information.

3) Not only linguistic competence is focused, learning strategy and cross-cultural competence are given their deserved importance as well.

These three points are in accordance with the earlier discussion on cross-cultural communicative competence. According to the tentative new model, cross-cultural communicative competence comprises not only communicative competence, but also cross-cultural competence, the former encompassing three components, namely, the linguistic, pragmatic and strategic competence. Unfortunately, in traditional EFL teaching and testing, linguistic competence has been given much more emphasis than the other components. This produced students who knew the language (the vocabulary, grammar and discourse) well, as is shown by the fact that most of Chinese college students passed the Band 4 or Band 6 college English test, but could not communicate appropriately in different sociolinguistic contexts or use communication strategies to compensate for breakdowns in cross-cultural communication.

To ensure that the test reveals the aim of teaching, firstly, pragmatic factors such as register and strategic factors should also be included the assessment criteria. Secondly, cross-cultural themes should be incorporated in SET design so as to measure candidates' cross-cultural competence.

2.6.2 Requirements for spoken English in CECR

The requirements for undergraduate College English teaching are set at three levels, i.e., basic requirements, intermediate requirements, and higher requirements. All non-English majors are required to attain to one of the three levels of requirements after studying and practicing English at school. The basic requirements, a goal that all college graduates must achieve, are meant for students who have or have not completed Band 7 of the Senior High School English Standards prior to entering college. Intermediate and higher requirements are respectively set for those who, having laid a good foundation of English, can afford time to learn more of the language, and have completed Bands 8 or 9 of the Senior High School English Standards upon entering college. The three levels of requirements, which incorporate knowledge and practical skills of the English language, learning strategies and intercultural communication, embody qualitatively and quantitatively the objective of College English teaching. (教育部高等教育司，2007：22-35)

The basic requirements are the minimum level that all non-English majors have to reach before graduation. Institutions of higher learning should set their own objectives in the light of their specific circumstances, strive to create favorable conditions, and encourage students to adjust their objectives in line with their own performance and try to meet the intermediate or higher requirements.

The three levels of requirements on speaking are set as follows:

Basic requirements

Students should be able to communicate in English in the course of learning, to conduct discussions on a given theme, and to talk about everyday topics with people from English-speaking countries. They should be able to give, after some preparation, short talks on familiar topics with clear articulation and basically correct pronunciation and intonation. They are expected to be able to use basic conversational strategies in dialogue. (教育部高等教育司，2007：22-35)

Intermediate requirements:

Students should be able to hold conversations in fairly fluent English

27

with people from English-speaking countries, and to employ fairly well conversational strategies. They should, by and large, be able to express their personal opinions, feelings and views, and to state facts, events and reasons with clear articulation and basically correct pronunciation and intonation. (教育部高等教育司，2007：22-35)

Higher Requirements:

Students should be able to conduct dialogues or discussions with certain degree of fluency and accuracy on general or specialized topics, and to make concise summaries of extended texts or speeches in difficult language. They should be able to deliver papers at academic conferences and participate in discussions. (教育部高等教育司，2007：22-35)

Table 2.2 summarizes the different dimensions of requirements for students' spoken English at different stages:

Interestingly, these requirements do not mention the cross-cultural dimension. This is probably because speaking English as a foreign language is cross-cultural by nature and because the communication in college English classrooms are basically pseudo-cross-cultural in that all the students and almost all the teachers are Chinese (although some English classes are taught by native speakers of English). This fact certainly adds up to the difficulty of cultivation of cross-cultural competence, but this does not necessarily devalue the importance of this dimension of competence.

These requirements should serve as a basis for constructing SEAT items.

Table 2.2 Dimensions of requirements of CECR on students' spoken English at different stages

Levels of requirements	Pronunciation and intonation	Activity types	Discourse level	Requirements on strategy	Pragmatic (contextual) dimension
Basic requirements	Basically correct	Discussions on a given theme Talks with native speakers of English about everyday topics Short talks on familiar topics after preparation	Short discourse level	Basic conversational strategies in dialogue	Classroom contexts

Intermediate requirements	Basically correct	Talks with native speakers of English about everyday topics personal opinions, feelings and views, and to state facts, events and reasons	Longer discourse level Fairly fluent English	fairly good use of conversational strategies	Social contexts
Higher requirements	Not specified	dialogues or discussions on general or specialized topics making concise summaries of extended text or speeches in difficult language Delivering papers at academic conferences and participating in discussions	Not specified	Not specified	Academic contexts

2.6.3 The functional requirements

In one of the appendixes, CECR also lists 27 functional requirements and useful expression for performing these functions, which should also be taken into consideration in designing an SEAT. They are greetings, introduction, farewells, thanks, apologies, invitation, asking for permission, wishes and congratulations, offering or asking for help, making appointments, making telephone calls, having meals, seeing the doctor, shopping, asking the way, talking about weather, advice and suggestions, showing attitude, expressing anger, expressing disappointment, expressing complaint, expressing sympathy, expressing encouragement, making a request, expressing surprise, expressing certainty or uncertainty, agreeing and disagreeing. (教育部高等教育司, 2007: 207-222)

2.7 A summary of this chapter

This chapter discusses more about "what" to test than about "how" to test spoken English in order to achieve high content validity and positive impact on teaching. It begins with a discussion on whether speaking is knowledge or skill, proceeds through the construction of a model of cross-cultural communicative competence, features of spoken language, the input and output hypotheses, the student-centered thematic model of EFL teaching, and finally to the requirements on spoken English in the CES.

The basic points can be summarized as follows:

1) Since speaking is regarded as a skill rather than knowledge, it can only be tested by actually facilitating the candidates to speak! This rules out the written format of SET. Moreover, if speaking as a skill is composed of the sub-skills of planning, selection and production, the rating criteria of a valid SET should also include not only accuracy, but also the production skills such as facilitation, compensation, and negotiation of meaning and even planning of what to speak.

2) As our goal of English teaching is to cultivate cross-cultural communicative competence, which is considered to encompass both communicative competence (linguistic, pragmatic and strategic) and cross-cultural competence (sensibility, tolerance and flexibility), the test of speaking should also include these components. Moreover, the strategic competence should include both language learning and language use strategies, therefore a good SET should encourage the strategies contributory to English learning and use while discouraging the noncontributory ones. Further, cross-cultural topics and input are preferable in an SET for the purpose of cultivating cross-cultural competence.

3) Spoken language displays some linguistic features such as adjustments, ellipsis and parataxis, repetition and formulaic expressions. Thus an SET should allow and even encourage these features to appear properly in candidates' speeches.

4) Because of the interdependent nature of language input and output, the optimal input or prompt for an achievement SET should be "adequate comprehensible linguistic input", which resembles those in teaching speaking as much as possible.

5) The "student-centered thematic model" of college English teaching has at least two implications for SET design. First, the candidate-centered testing formats or techniques such as presentation, discussion, and role-play are more favorable than the more tester-centered ones such as interviews (unless the candidate plays the role of the interviewer). Second, the testing activities should be centered on one theme.

6) The SEAT should be in consistence with the requirements of spoken English in CES. It should select the test formats which resemble the activity types regulated for different stages of college English education, focusing more on the longer discourse level oral

communication activities such as discussion and presentation, etc. Meanwhile, it should take into account the functional and notional requirements.

Chapter 3 Language testing theories and their implications for the SEAT design

As was mentioned in the beginning of part two, if chapter 2 deals with "what" should be tested in the SEAT, then this chapter will discuss "how" the SEAT should be tested. For this purpose, we will look at the mainstream language testing theories. We will highlight the theory of communicative language testing because of its dominance in today's language testing.

3.1 Characteristics of communicative language testing

Judging from the theoretical model on which it is based, the history of language testing has roughly undergone three stages, i.e., the pre-scientific testing, the psychometirc-structuralist testing, and the communicative language testing. In the pre-scientific stage language was taught and hence tested as knowledge and the test design was solely based on the teacher/tester's experience without any scientific analysis. The psychometric-structuralist testing started in 1940s, and is still influential. It is based upon a structuralist view of language and a behaviorist view of learning (stimulus-response theory). It believes that language can be divided into skills (listening, speaking, reading and writing) and knowledge (phonetics, grammar and vocabulary). Consequently, it adopts the discrete-point test, in which each item is supposed to test only one single element of a linguistic skill (韩宝成, 2000: 47-52).

Communicative language testing can also be referred to as "psycholinguistic-sociolinguistic testing". It started in 1960s, and represents the trend of language testing. It is concerned primarily (if not totally) with how language is used in communication. Consequently, most communicative language tests aim to incorporate tasks which approximate as closely as possible to those in real life. Success is judged in terms of the effectiveness of communication rather than formal linguistic accuracy. The models of communicative competence discussed in Chapter 2 represent part of the theoretical background of communicative language testing, which aims to test the communicative competence rather than merely linguistic competence.

Drawing upon the test of the Communicative Use of English as a

Foreign Language (CUEFL) conducted by the University of Cambridge Local Examinations Syndicate (UCLES), 贾志高 (1998: 37) briefly summarized Weir's views (Weir, 1990) of characteristics of communicative language testing. These characteristics are listed as follows:

1) Task-based testing items

2) Authentic materials in listening and reading tests

3) Use of language under the constraints of situations, socio-cultures, affections and functions

4) Interactiveness of SET

5) Validity focused

6) Adoption of degree of skill instead of marks.

The SEAT to be designed in the present study is intended to test the cross-cultural communicative competence of Chinese English learners in speaking. Thus it should adopt the communicative language testing approach. As mentioned above, a good achievement test should reflect the particular approach to teaching. In China, the dominant approach to English teaching is the communicative approach. Therefore, the SEAT to be designed should reveal the above six characteristics. To be specific, the SEAT should be able to

1) provide a task or tasks for candidates to perform;

2) supply authentic linguistic input (written or spoken) prior to their performance;

3) design the task and the linguistic input of cross-cultural topics;

4) encourage interaction among candidates;

5) ensure high validity;

6) assess candidates by way of a degree of skills.

3.2 Principles for language test development and use

Different scholars have established different criteria for judging whether a language test is "good" or not (Heaton, 1988; Bachman & Palmer, 1996; Underhill, 1987; 桂诗春, 1986; 刘润清, 1991; 舒运祥, 1999; etc). Bachman and Palmer's (1996) model is discussed here, because it is presented on the basis of practical research. According to Bachman and

Palmer (1996: 9-42), two principles have to be observed in language test development and use. They are termed as "the correspondence principle" and the "usefulness principle".

3.2.1 The correspondence principle

This principle refers to the need for a correspondence between language test performance and language use. As Bachman and Palmer state: "In order for a particular language test to be useful for its intended purposes, test performance must correspond in demonstrable ways to language use in non-test situations" (Bachman & Palmer, 1996: 9). They have constructed a framework to demonstrate this relationship (see figure 3.1).

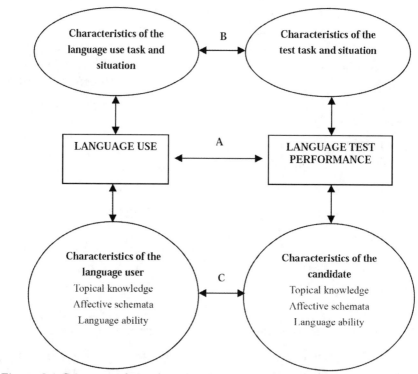

Figure 3.1 Correspondence between language use and language test performance (Bachman & Palmer, 1996: 12)

As indicated above, the correspondence between language use and language test performance is of central concern in designing, developing, and using language tests (illustrated by the horizontal arrow labeled 'A' in figure 3.1). In order to demonstrate this correspondence, we need to be able to demonstrate the correspondence between the characteristics of the situation and tasks in language use and those of the situation and tasks in language test (illustrated by the arrow labeled 'B' in figure 3.1), and the correspondence between the characteristics of individuals as language users and those of the candidates (illustrated by the arrow labeled 'C' in figure 3.1).

3.2.2 The usefulness principle

According to Bachman and Palmer (1996: 18), the test usefulness can be expressed in figure 3.2.

Usefulness = Reliability + Construct validity + Authenticity + Interactiveness + Impact + Practicality

Figure 3.2 SET Usefulness (Adapted from figure 2.1 from Bachman & Palmer, 1996: 18)

Bachman and Palmer's three principles for operationalizing test usefulness are as follows (Bachman & Palmer, 1996: 18):

Principles for operationalizing test usefulness

Principle 1	It is the overall usefulness of the test that is to be maximized rather than the individual qualities that affect usefulness.
Principle 2	The individual test qualities cannot be evaluated independently, but must be evaluated in terms of their combined effect on the overall usefulness of the test.
Principle 3	Test usefulness and the appropriate balance among the different qualities cannot be prescribed in general, but must be determined for each specific testing situation.

While reliability and construct validity are two basic concepts familiar to both language testers and language teachers, the other four qualities are somewhat less familiar, thus deserve some discussion here.

A. Authenticity

As argued in the discussion about the correspondence principle, in order to justify the use of language tests, we need to be able to demonstrate that performance on language tests corresponds to language use in specific domains other than the language test itself. One aspect of demonstrating this pertains to the correspondence between the characteristics of TLU (target language use) tasks and test task. Thus, *authenticity* can be defined as the degree of correspondence between the characteristics of given language test task and the features of TLU task (see figure 3.3).

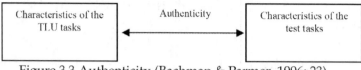

Figure 3.3 Authenticity (Bachman & Parmer, 1996: 23)

Therefore, before the design of the achievement SET, a needs analysis and a study of the CECR should be done to identify characteristics of the TLU tasks in order to achieve authenticity of the test.

B. Interactiveness

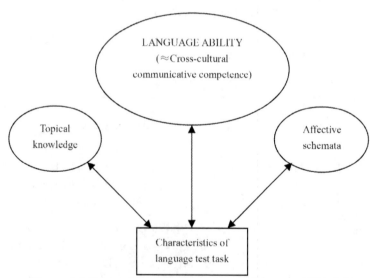

Figure 3.4 Interactiveness (Bachman & Parmer, 1996: 26)

The concept of interactiveness may be a little confusing. It may denote, for some people, the interactiveness among candidates or between candidates and testers of a test task. However, Bachman and Palmer (1996: 25) define *interactiveness* as the extent and type of involvement of the candidate's individual characteristics in accomplishing a test task. The individual characteristics that are most relevant to language testing are the candidate's language ability (roughly the equivalent of the
36

above-mentioned cross-cultural communicative competence), topical knowledge, and affective schemata. Thus, the interactiveness of a given test task can thus be represented in figure 3.4.

Thus, to achieve high interactiveness, the test designer should take into consideration not only learners' cross-cultural communicative competence, but also the topical knowledge and affective schemata.

C. Impact

Another quality of language tests is their impact on society, educational systems, and upon the individuals within those systems. The impact of test use operates at two levels: a micro level, in terms of the individuals who are affected by the particular test use, and a macro level, in terms of the educational system or society. Impact can be represented as in Figure 3.5.

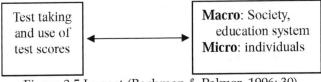

Figure 3.5 Impact (Bachman & Palmer, 1996: 30)

Another term related to impact is often referred to as backwash (or washback) effect. However, Bachman and Palmer (1996: 30) regard this concept as an aspect of impact. To be particular, backwash effect refers to the impact of a test on the process of learning and teaching. In this study, the impact on society is considered a question of little value; therefore, the terms of impact and backwash/washback effect are exchangeable in this book.

It has long been agreed that the SEAT is essential due to its backwash effect. As Heaton (1988: 170) points out: "... in spite of possible unreliability, oral tests should be continued as far as possible in certain language learning situations if for no other reason than the backwash effects they have on the teaching that takes place before the test".

Further, backwash effect should not only be a reason for SET, it is also one of the basic considerations during the construction of SET. For example, the written indirect SET format mentioned in Chapter 2 is likely to have negative impact on teaching because it may mislead the teaching of speaking toward the conception of regarding it as knowledge rather than a skill.

D. Practicality

Perhaps the biggest issue to be considered in the SEAT to be constructed is practicality. This is because SET has always been considered expensive and time-consuming, while the teaching situation does not allow much resource to be used on an achievement test. Even in the large-scale nationwide proficiency SET of CET, only a minority of college English learners, i.e., the students who score higher than 85 in band 4 and 75 in band 6, have the privilege of being given an opportunity.

We can define practicality as the relationship between the resources that will be required in the design, development, and use of the test and the resources that will be available for these activities. This relationship can be represented as in Figure 3.6.

Practicality = Available resources / Required resources

If practicality ≥1,the test development and use is practical.

If practicality <1, the test development and use is not practical.

Figure 3.6 Practicality (Bachman & Palmer, 1996: 36)

Practicality is the extent to which the demands of the particular test specifications can be met within the limits of existing resources. We believe this view of practicality is useful because it enables us to define a 'threshold level' for practicality in any given testing situation. If the resources demands of the test specifications do not exceed the available resources at any stage in test development, then the test is practical, and test development and use can proceed. If available resources are exceeded, then the test is not practical and the developer must either modify the specifications to reduce the resources required, or increase the available resources or reallocate them so that they can be utilized more efficiently. Thus, a practical test is one whose design, development, and use do not require more resources than are available.

According to Bachman and Palmer, resources can be classified into three types (see figure 3.7).

In our case of the SEAT, the resources are very scarce. Although material resources can be easily available, the human resources and time for administering the test are very limited. What makes it even more difficult is the tight budget. The university is not prepared to spend much money on this test, while collecting money from students, as is practiced by CET-SET, is considered inappropriate. Since almost no money is available, the test for each class is assumed to be administered within four class hours and to be administered, assessed, and reported by the English teachers. (Of course, the class teachers could shift their students to avoid bias if necessary.)

1	**Human resources**
	(e.g. test writers, scorers or raters, test administrators, and clerical support)
2	**Material resources**
	Space (e.g. rooms for test development and test administration)
	Equipment (e.g. typewriters, word processors, tape and video recorders, computers)
	Materials (e.g. paper, pictures, library resources)
3	**Time**
	Development time (time from the beginning of the test development process to the reporting of scores from the first operational administration)
	Time for specific tasks (e.g. designing, writing, administering, scoring, analyzing)

Figure 3.7 Types of resources (Bachman & Palmer, 1996: 37)

An issue within the consideration of practicality is *administrative feasibility*. It means that if the achievement SET is intended to be practical, it should also be as easy as possible to administrate. For example, the candidates should be randomly selected for each assessor or assessors if the reporting of scores is supposed to be norm-referenced to achieve better reliability (文秋芳，1999: 115). This consideration might be attractive, but it adds much more effort to administration.

In order to be more specific about practicality, a concept for measuring time consumption of the examiners/assessors, i.e., teacher time on each student (TT/S), is introduced here. This is done because in our case the scarcest resource is qualified teachers. For example, if a 15-ninute interview (as that used in the test for Certificate of Proficiency in English (CPE)) is adopted, the time consumption on the teacher would be incredibly huge. In a normal Chinese university, a teacher of English usually teaches more than 3 classes, with each class consisting of approximately 40 students. The teacher's time consumption can be easily calculated as follows:

Time consumption of one teacher

=15 minutes * 40 students * 3 classes

=1800 minutes

= 30 hours

What does 30 hours mean? It means 4 full working days, and more than one third of a teacher's teaching hours of a semester (90 class hours, each class hour is 45 minutes long). Spending such a large portion of teachers' work time in assessing students' oral achievement is impractical.

Then how much time is considered acceptable? In negotiating with both the teachers and administrators of the department, it is found that the SEAT should be done in no more than 4 class hours (preferably within 2 class hours) for each class. The teacher time for each student is then calculated in this way:

$$TT/C \in [2\,h, 4\,h]$$

$$TT/C \in [90\,min, 180\,min]$$

$$TT/S \in [90\,min/40, 180\,min/40]$$

$$TT/S \in [2.25\,min, 4.5\,min]$$

Note: TT/C = teacher time per class, TT/S = teacher time per student, h = hour(s), min = minute(s)

This means that each student should finish his or her SEAT between 2.25 minutes and 4.5 minutes. This length is certainly too short for an interview between the examiner and the candidate. Therefore, the candidate-centered SET activity is favored for two reasons:

1) This type of activity resembles the major classroom activities conducted in Zhejiang University and other colleges using the New College English textbook series, which is developed according to a "student-centered thematic approach". Thus, this format has preferable impact on classroom teaching.

2) This SEAT format can be executed within the acceptable amount of time. If the test is given in a learner-centered group activity of four students, the task should be finished between 10 minutes to 18 minutes. This is feasible.

But can a sample of speech of between 2.25 to 4.5 minutes reveal the communicative competence of learners? The empirical research reported in chapter 5 and 6 is carried out to attempt an answer to this question.

3.3 Test types

After a brief discussion of the principles for the development and administration of a test and their implications for the SEAT to be designed, it is now necessary to decide what type of tests is to be designed. SET can be classified into different categories judging from different criteria. Four important criteria are provided in table 3.1.

Table 3.1 Types of SET

Criteria for classification	Test types
Usage	Achievement, proficiency, aptitude and diagnosis
Channel (whether the assessor is face to face with the candidate)	Direct, semi-direct and indirect (machine-mediated)
Aim of testing	Criterion-referenced and norm-referenced
Scoring method	Holistic and analytical

3.3.1 Achievement, proficiency, aptitude or diagnosis?

According to Heaton (1988: 171-173), most specialists agree that language tests can be classified into four types according to the usage of the tests: achievement/attainment tests, proficiency tests, aptitude/prognostic tests and diagnostic tests. They are summarized in table 3.2.

Table 3.2 Test types

Test types		Descriptions	Examples
achievement /attainment tests	Class progress tests	➢ Designed to measure the extent to which the students have mastered the material taught in the classroom; ➢ Based on the language program; ➢ Backwash effect on teaching motivation being important features; ➢ Should encourage the students to perform well in the target language and to gain additional confidence (scores on it should be high). ➢ Designers are the teachers of the class	Dictation of words learnt in the previous lessons
	Achievement tests	➢ Far more formal than progress tests; ➢ Intended to measure achievement on a large scale; ➢ Syllabus-based; ➢ Designers not necessarily class teachers; ➢ Should reflect the particular approach to learning and teaching that has previously been adopted	Annual school examinations
proficiency tests		➢ Aimed to define a student's language proficiency with reference to a particular task (e.g. to go to a university in the target language country) which he or she will be required to perform; ➢ Not related to any syllabus or teaching program;	TOEFL
Aptitude/prognostic tests		➢ Designed to measure the student's probable performance in a foreign language which he or she has not started to learn; ➢ Consisting the element of intelligence, age, motivation, memory, phonological sensitivity, and sensitivity to grammatical patterning; ➢ Seeking to predict the student's probable strengths and weaknesses in learning a foreign language by measuring performance in an artificial language	
diagnostic tests		➢ To diagnose areas of difficulty so that appropriate remedial action can be taken later. ➢ Few tests are constructed solely as diagnostic tests. Achievement and proficiency tests are frequently used for this purpose.	Phoneme discrimination tests, grammar and usage tests

The SET to be constructed is basically an achievement test since it is far more formal in that it is intended to go with the written achievement test, to be held on a large scale once a semester (or once in a year in some cases), to be consistent with the syllabus, and to reflect the approach adopted in teaching.

3.3.2 Direct, semi-direct or indirect (machine-mediated)?

Direct SET is a traditional test type. In a direct test, the assessor scores the candidate face to face. Indirect SET is a test type in which the performance of candidates is recorded in a language laboratory and is scored later by the assessor. A semi-direct SET is a test type in which the examiner and candidates communicate face to face and the process is recorded thoroughly, while the assessment takes place later by the assessor via the tape rather than on the spot. The advantages and disadvantages are discussed in table 3.3.

Based on the table 3.3, the following implications can be drawn:

1) Since practicality is of basic concern in an achievement SET (which will be discussed in the coming sections), semi-direct SET is excluded in our case.

2) As for an achievement test, the authenticity and impact are even more important to some degree than reliability, direct SET is the favored format.

3) Much effort, especially in the training of assessors, should be done to improve reliability of direct SET.

4) However, the indirect SET deserves research effort so that a comparison can be made with the direct SET.

Table 3.3 Advantages and disadvantages of direct, semi-direct or indirect (machine-mediated) SET

Test types	Advantages	Disadvantages
Direct SET	➢ The assessor can observe facial expressions and body languages of the candidates, which is also considered factors attributing to communicative competence. ➢ The assessor can remind the candidates if they speak too little or in a voice too low to be heard clearly. ➢ The face-to-face communication enables relatively high authenticity and face validity.	➢ Training of a large number of assessors is expensive and time-consuming. ➢ Examiners/assessors' linguistic competence and affective factors (e.g. mood) may affect the performance of candidates.
Semi-direct SET	➢ Semi-direct SET has all the advantages of direct SET. ➢ The recorded tape can be reassessed to improve reliability.	➢ Semi-direct SET has all the disadvantages of direct SET. ➢ It is even more expensive and time-consuming in that the administration and assessment are done separately and thus the cost is doubled.
Indirect SET	➢ The examiner does not affect candidates' performance. ➢ All the candidates receive exactly the same linguistic input, thus this may be fairer to them. ➢ The assessment is not affected by candidates' appearance.	➢ The laboratory setting and man to machine communication are not authentic. ➢ Assessment is impossible in case that the candidate speaks very little or that the recording is unclear. ➢ The assessment costs as much as direct SET in that the assessors have to listen to all the recordings of candidates. ➢ The feasibility of this test format is dependent on accessibility of enough large language laboratories.

3.3.3 Criteria-referenced or norm-referenced?

The distinction between criteria-referenced SET and norm-referenced SET is highly aim-oriented. The former is aimed to judge which level the candidates have reached, while the latter is intended to locate the relative position of one candidate among all the examinees. Furthermore, the norm-referenced SET takes it as a prerequisite that the candidates are randomly sampled to be scored by assessors.

3.3.4 Scoring method: holistic or analytical?

The marking of SET can be holistic or analytical. Holistic marking is also called impressionistic marking. Adopting this method, the assessor scores candidates according to his/her overall impression of the candidates' performance against a general description of levels. Analytical marking usually requires specific descriptions of a list of marking categories such as pronunciation and intonation, vocabulary size, grammar, fluency, etc. In this way, the assessor marks candidates' performance against the descriptions of the different marking categories and gives separate scores for separate categories. Sometimes different weightings are given to different categories according to the purpose of the SET and opinions of test experts.

Both marking methods have their advantages and disadvantages (see table 3.4).

Table 3.4 Advantages and disadvantages of holistic and analytical marking methods

Marking methods	Advantages	Disadvantages
Analytical	➤ High reliability ➤ Scores can be used for diagnostic purpose.	➤ More burden on the part of the assessor since he/she has to produce several scores
Holistic	➤ Efficient	➤ Reliability doubtful

Since our achievement SET is intended to achieve positive impact on teaching and learning, analytical marking method is preferred. Another advantage of this method is that it achieves better reliability, which is also an issue of great concern for SET as a subjective test.

3.4 Elicitation techniques for SET: strengths and limitations

After a discussion of some critical theoretical issues relevant to SET, it is now appropriate to look into SET in a more specific way. Underhill (1987: 44-87) puts forward more than sixty elicitation techniques and variations for SET. Although, as he points out, "there is no natural classification of test techniques", it is beneficial to look into and comment on these techniques prior to the design of our achievement SET.

Underhill "arbitrarily" identified 20 techniques, each having some variations. In the following text, a brief description of some techniques is given together with my comments. However, some of these techniques are ruled out in our discussion either because they are too easy for Chinese learners of English at the college level (e.g. form-filling, making appropriate responses, learner-learner description and re-creation) or because they are not communicative or authentic (e.g. reading aloud, reading blank dialogues) or both (e.g. question and answer, sentence completion from aural or written stimulus, sentence correction, sentence transformation, sentence repetition).

3.4.1 Discussion / conversation

According to Underhill, this technique involves a conversation between the examiner and the candidate on a topic of common interest in a relaxed atmosphere. To somebody outside the conversation, it is hard to distinguish it from an interview (see 3.4.5). The difference is one of attitude or intention, rather than technique: in a discussion /conversation, the examiner keeps overall control, but is willing and able to yield the initiative to the candidate to steer the conversation or bring up a new topic. More accurately, the topics discussed and the directions taken by the conversation are the result of the interaction between the people, involved in a kind of negotiation below the surface level of the words. Tone of voice, pitch and intonation, and expressions of face and body language all contribute to this negotiation. These are features of natural conversation which make this procedure, when it succeeds, authentic and communicative (Underhill, 1987: 45-46).

This technique is useful due to its good validity, authenticity, interactiveness and impact. But it seems to be very time-consuming because one candidate is examined at a time. If the examiner and the
46

assessor are the same person, this would make the communication unnatural and thus affect the candidate's performance. Also, it can make the examiner and assessor too busy. If the examiner and the assessor are different people, then this test would become even more unfeasible for a large-scale test.

To make it practical in our situation, the discussion could be among several candidates, while the examiner's task may as well be reduced to just keeping the test procedure going while focusing on the assessment.

3.4.2 Oral report/presentation

The candidate prepares and gives an oral presentation lasting from five to ten minutes. He/she is expected to refer to notes, but reading aloud is strongly discouraged. The use of simple aids such as an overhead projector, blackboard or flipchart diagrams is encouraged if appropriate. At the end of the presentation, the speaker is expected to deal with some questions. Making presentations is an authentic and communicative activity both for professional and academic purposes (Underhill, 1987: 47-49).

When this technique is used, the choice of the topic is very important. The topic should be relevant to the aims of the program or the needs of the learners and should contain new information or put forward a new point of view. It should not be so specialized that only the speaker himself is interested in, nor should it be so general that it has no apparent purpose other than as a language exercise. Ideally, the topic should be chosen by the learner in consultation with his teacher who will help match the ability of the learner with the difficulty of a given topic (Underhill, 1987: 47).

Particularly when giving presentations is an authentic activity for the learners, specific mark categories can be used for the different functional skills involved, for example, explaining factual data, expressing opinions or arguments, dealing with questions, summarizing, and so on. In this way, the candidates' particular weaknesses can be identified. Where the presentation is given to an audience, the assessor will be able to back up her own impressions by watching the effect the speaker has on the listeners in terms of their comprehension, their reactions, and their questions (Underhill, 1987: 47-48).

This technique is highly valid, interactive, and also can be very practical. One other advantage is that this technique enables candidates to display their linguistic competence not only at sentence level, but also on discourse level, which is considered essential for learners at tertiary level.

One possible problem with this technique is that if the candidates choose the topic several days or weeks before the test, then some would play safe to choose some familiar topics with no challenge at all. Some may even plagiarize a speech or composition from somewhere or ask other people to compose one for them. Some may rehearse while others don't before the test. However, if the topic is given to them five or ten minutes before the test, it may make them nervous. If the topic is unfamiliar to them, they may even be at loss as to what to say.

Of course, a list of topics can be given for them to choose from. In this case, several lists have to be prepared in advance to prevent two candidates from selecting the same topic. Otherwise, one candidate may take advantage of another by repeating what he has already said.

One other problem with this topic-based technique is that it does not reflect what happens in real life, nor does it reflect the requirements in the syllabus and the most common classroom activities. Seldom is a person required to give a formal presentation without some linguistic input in our life, although some input might have been given long before the speech. In academic situations, when one is to give a presentation, he or she usually reviews a huge bunch of literature in the field. In the syllabus, the requirement for spoken English is highly input-based (see 2.6.2). In the student-centered thematic approach, speaking activities are also input-based. Actually, it is hard to imagine how speaking ability can develop without linguistic input listening and reading.

Thus, for the benefit of authenticity and backwash effect, providing candidates with a reasonable amount of linguistic input should preferably modify the oral report/presentation technique of SET. Of course, in such a case, proper instructions have to be given to prevent candidates from reading or reciting the given materials.

3.4.3 Learner-learner joint discussion/decision making

When this technique is used, a group of two or more learners are tested together, without the participation of an interviewer. The learners have to maintain and direct the discussion entirely on their own. The task usually involves using information from written documents and coming to a decision or consensus about certain questions through group discussion. Where several documents or sources are used, these can be read before the discussion begins, or even at a previous stage in a test battery. Since it is

48

the discussion, rather than the final decision, that is the important feature, there is usually no single correct answer; otherwise, having reached a conclusion, the learners will tend to sit back and wait rather than continue talking. Learners are told beforehand that the assessment will be based on the way they express and justify their opinions, and evaluate those of others, rather than just on the factual content of what they say. The discussion can be marked live or be taped for later marking (Underhill, 1987: 49).

This technique is the most favored form of the intended SEAT for it meets almost all the requirements of a useful test in our situation. It is especially preferable in terms of practicality and backwash effect, which are two vital qualities in our concern about an SEAT. It is very practical because it allows testing of as many as three or four students at the same time. It is likely to have positive impact on teaching because it is one of the most commonly used activities in the student-centered classrooms in Zhejiang University and many other universities and colleges in China. Moreover, Learner-learner joint type makes more interaction among the test takers as well as the interaction between the raters and test-takers. The test takers in such test are more active that the other types of test (杨莉芳,2006:42-48).

One possible problem with this technique is that the discussion may not be able to go on if the candidates are very different in terms of linguistic competence. For example, one candidate might claim that he couldn't understand another because of poor pronunciation and intonation of the speaker.

Fortunately, this is not likely to happen in our case. In order to cater to the needs of students of different levels, the English classes in Zhejiang University, (and also in many other colleges and universities), are arranged at four bands according to students' English levels. This means that in each class, all the students are within the same band, and therefore are somewhat similar in overall language proficiency. Although there is some difference in their oral competence, (this presumably is one precondition why SET is necessary), this difference is not so large as to make the communication impossible. Second, the candidates often perform learner-learner joint discussion in the classroom.

3.4.4 Role-play

In a role-play, according to Underhill, the learner is asked to take on a particular role in a particular situation. He has to converse with the examiner in a way that is appropriate to the role and the situation given (Underhill, 1987: 51-54). However, this notion is expanded here because the candidate does not have to role-play with the examiner. One alternative format within this technique is that two or even more candidates play different roles together, meanwhile the examiner may play one role, or may stand back as the assessor only.

This technique, especially the alternative form in which the examiner stand back, is also one of the possible forms of our SEAT for its preferable validity, authenticity, interactiveness, impact and practicality.

However, a possible problem is personal reluctance to participate. Role-playing, by definition, implies pretending to be someone other than one really is. Some people can do this more easily than others. In some cultures, role-playing may be seen as unusual and therefore unsettling behavior, especially in an educational context. Some individuals are personally unhappy about pretending to be someone else, and any attempt at persuasion may only increase this unease. Therefore, there are both cultural and individual differences among people in their ability to role-play, which do not necessarily reflect differences in language proficiency (Underhill, 1987: 52-53).

3.4.5 Interview

The interview is the most common elicitation technique in oral tests; for many people, it is the only kind of technique. It is a direct, face-to-face exchange between the candidate and the examiner. It follows a pre-determined structure, but still allows both people a degree of freedom to say what they genuinely think (Underhill, 1987: 54).

There are three problems with the technique of interview.

Firstly, oral interviews might not be practical in our situation, because one assessor can only interview one candidate at a time.

Secondly, this technique does not reflect the student-centered communicative approach adopted in the teaching practice in China's universities.

Finally, according Underhill (1987: 56), oral interviews often fail to discriminate effectively at higher levels. As he argues:

The oral interview technique is well-suited for testing learners at the intermediate level and below, where detailed rating scales present easily-recognizable learner profiles; but at higher levels it is difficult to produce such well-defined scales, and the usual mark categories fail to discriminate well (Underhill, 1987: 56).

However, oral interview is not totally unusable provided that not many candidates are tested and that the examiner knows the constraints of this technique. As Underhill remarks:

The tightly-controlled interview that is more like a question and answer test will not easily elicit the learner's best language performance, and it is therefore more important at higher levels that the interviewer stand back a little and allow the learner to display his conversational fluency skills. (Underhill, 1987: 56).

3.4.6 Using a picture or picture story

Before the test starts, the learner is given a picture or sequence of pictures to look at. Then the examiner asks the learner to describe the picture and allows him to speak freely. When the learner has finished speaking, or if he falters, the interviewer may ask pre-designed questions to elicit particular information, perhaps about a point the learner has missed or has not made clear (Underhill, 1987: 66).

Generally speaking, visual stimuli are an economic and effective way of providing a topic of conversation without giving the learner words and phrases to manipulate and give back. It is also an excellent technique to be used at the beginning of an SET in which a sequence of test techniques is used, and can be used just as warm-up, lasting perhaps one or two minutes, without any formal marks being awarded. Although there is some freedom of expression, the topic of conversation is fixed by the picture(s).

There are some limitations to this technique. Firstly, with a visual stimulus, there is a danger that the candidate will miss the point of a picture or story for personal or cultural reasons. For example, some humor for one culture is unattainable for another, while candidates from the countryside may not be able to understand a picture or story about city life.

Also, unless vocabulary items in the picture are supplied, candidates who know the names of two or three crucial items will be at a strong advantage over those who do not. Even if the items are supplied on request, and marks not deducted, it is psychologically de-motivating for candidates to have to ask for vocabulary in a test.

Moreover, suitable cartoon stories are hard to find and difficult for an amateur to draw. Particularly in situations where learners can and will discuss with each other details of the test, it may be necessary to find several alternative pictures or stories to use in rotation.

Finally there is the problem of the possible effects on teaching. Pictures as stimulus for speaking are simply very rare in an English textbook for college students. Comparatively, linguistic input, whether in sound or textual forms, is the dominant form of stimulus for speaking activities. Therefore, there seems to be little need for designing an achievement SET with visual stimuli.

3.4.7 Giving instructions/description/explanation

When this technique is used, with minimal preparation, the learner is to describe, at some length, a well-known object, a system or an everyday procedure. The description is factual and the object being described is widely known. Choosing something that is familiar to every body is a good way of getting the learner to produce connected discourse on a given topic. At the same time, it allows considerable freedom of choice of expression without requiring extensive preparation. Normally, the learner is given a list of about six topics to choose from and a few minutes' preparation time (Underhill, 1987: 69). Some examples of suitable topics are:

- How do you make a good cup of tea or coffee?

- Describe a bicycle.

- Describe how to prepare a favorite dish.

- Give instructions for using a public pay phone.

- Explain how you would advise someone to look for a job.

- Describe how people celebrate the New Year.

This technique seems very similar to oral report/presentation. The only difference might be one of difficulty because it involves very familiar objects or topics and does not require so much preparation but oral report requires more thorough preparation on a more specialized subject.

3.4.8 Précis or re-telling story or text from aural stimulus

The learner hears a short passage or story on a tape. He is then asked to re-tell the passage or to summarize it. The instructions usually emphasize that it is the quality, rather than the quantity, of the re-telling that is important; and that as far as possible he should use his own words rather than try to recall exact phrases from the passage. These points are usually reinforced by the marking system, which rewards good paraphrase and reproduction of the main idea of the story or passage (Underhill, 1987: 71).

This technique has good validity, authenticity, interactiveness, impact and practicality. It might even be carried out in a language laboratory setting. Moreover, it displays competence at the discourse rather than sentence level.

Some people might doubt the validity of this technique and argue that since this is a mixed skill test, it might not be testing speaking but listening instead. But, as Underhill (1987: 71) remarks, "clearly, speaking is rarely used in real life without listening also being involved, so it is, in that sense, authentic." Judging from language acquisition process (the input and output hypotheses) and the impact factor, the inclusion of listening might even be an advantage of this technique. Of course, listening materials should be within candidates' linguistic competence and topical knowledge.

3.4.9 Re-telling a story from written stimulus

The candidate reads a passage or a series of short passages and is asked to re-tell each one in his own words immediately afterwards. There is no fixed time limit for the reading stage, but the candidate is not allowed to refer back to the written text once he has begun to re-tell the story or text. Thus the candidate is usually given the text to read at the beginning stage of the test, and the examiner then takes the text back once the learner indicates that he has finished reading it. In this case, the recall is immediate. Alternatively, it is possible to delay the recall by carrying out some intervening activity between the reading and re-telling stages in order to accentuate the importance of memory and mental organization (Underhill, 1987: 73-74).

This technique is only slightly different from the précis or re-telling story or text from aural stimulus. Thus the advantages and disadvantages of both techniques are almost the same.

3.4.10 Translating/interpreting

When this technique is used, both the examiner and the candidate have in front of them a native-language text the learner is familiar with. The interviewer chooses a short passage, or a series of passages, from the text and asks the learner to translate it into the foreign language. In the marking system, attention is paid both to the accuracy and the style. Familiarity with the content of the passage is essential if the learner is expected to be sensitive to nuances of style and register (Underhill, 1987: 79).

Translation is often regarded as old-fashioned and unsuitable for use in programs where so-called direct method teaching is used. Translating well is a different skill from speaking well in the foreign language. Therefore, it does not on its own make a satisfactory test of oral ability.

However, it is a quick and easy test to administer, and can conveniently be planned into a sequence of test techniques. It can follow on naturally from reading aloud and lead into re-telling a written story (see 3.4.9). Although a teaching program will probably aim to get learners to think in the foreign language, and not translate all the time, interpreting or translating tasks are very authentic and can be made communicative.

3.4.11 A summary of SET techniques

Finally, a decision should be made on which techniques discussed above can be used in our SET. For the sake of practicality and the consideration of the candidate-centeredness, the techniques should be suitable for group activities among learners, during which the examiner/assessor's task is reduced to ensuring the process and marking the candidates. This rules out the interview technique. The evaluation of the remaining ones is summarized in table 3.5.

Table 3.5 Evaluation of SET elicitation techniques

Techniques	Advantages	Disadvantages	Is it suitable for our SET?	Possible improvement
Discussion / conversation	good validity, authenticity, interactiveness and impact	time-consuming thus impractical	Yes	The discussion could be among several candidates.
Oral report/ presentation	valid, interactive, and practical display linguistic competence at discourse level	Just providing the topic makes it unreliable, inauthentic, produce negative on impact	Yes	Provide essential linguistic input to the candidates.
Learner-learner joint discussion/ decision making	meet almost all the requirements of a useful test in our situation.	not suitable for candidates whose linguistic competence vary enormously	Yes	Group candidates with similar linguistic competence together by the result of a written test if possible.
Role-play	preferable validity, authenticity, interactiveness, impact and practicality	personal reluctance to participate	Yes	Create roles desirable for candidates.
Using a picture or picture story	economic and effective way of providing a topic	A visual stimulus can be misunderstood. possible unfairness. poor practicality and impact	No	
Giving instructions /description /explanation	similar to oral report/presentation			
Précis or re-tell story or text from aural stimulus	good validity, authenticity, interactiveness, impact and practicality	too difficult aural input may affect validity	yes	choosing listening materials within candidates' linguistic competence and topical knowledge
Re-telling a story from written stimulus	similar to précis or re-telling story or text from aural stimulus			
Translating/ interpreting	good authenticity, practicality	poor impact and validity.	No	

It should be pointed out here that an SET is likely to be a combination of two or more elicitation techniques to achieve authenticity, fairness, balance and flexibility (Underhill, 1987: 38).

3.5 A theoretical model for the procedure of constructing an SET

文秋芳(1999: 97) puts forward a theoretical model for the procedure of constructing an SET. However, she didn't take authenticity and interactiveness into consideration in the model. This is probably because she included these two qualities in the concept of "validity". But as these qualities are considered to be more specific than the terms of "face validity" and "content validity", they are added into the model in the present study. Thus the model could be modified as in figure 3.8.

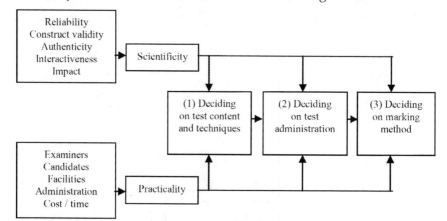

Figure 3.8 A theoretical model for the procedure of constructing an SET

(adapted from 文秋芳, 1999: 97)

3.6 A summary of this chapter

This chapter deals with "how" to conduct an SEAT with relevance to communicative language testing theories. First, it discusses the characteristics of communicative approach to language testing against psychometric-structuralist approach. Second, it refers to Bachman and Palmer's principles for language test development and use. Then, it tries to decide what type of tests our intended SEAT is. Finally, it comments on some elicitation techniques. From the discussion of this chapter, the following points can be summarized.

1)   The achievement SET should provide authentic test task and linguistic

input of cross-cultural topics and should endeavor to encourage interaction among candidates.

2) The test task should be based upon a needs analysis in order to achieve correspondence between characteristics of test performance and those of language use. Meanwhile, the test should satisfy the qualities of a "useful test".

3) The intended SET is an achievement test in nature. A direct, criteria-referenced SET is favored for our purpose, and an analytical marking method is preferable to a holistic one.

4) Discussion/conversation, oral report/presentation, learner-learner joint discussion/decision making, role-play, giving instruction/description/explanation, and story-retelling from aural or written stimulus are applicable elicitation techniques for our purpose. However, improvement has to be made to some of them.

5) A theoretical model for the procedure of constructing an SET is presented by adapting one built up by the earlier researchers.

Chapter 4 A contrastive study of several SET formats

In this chapter, several recognized SET formats will be examined in the hope to get some inspiration for our practice. These SET formats are carefully chosen to represent the mainstream in the United Kingdom, the United States, Hong Kong, and Mainland China. Moreover, these tests are all intended for adult candidates and, to some degree, for a similar purpose, i.e., to measure whether or not the candidates can perform authentic tasks in English. The tests to be examined are Oral Interaction for Communicative Use of English as a Foreign Language (CUEFL-Oral Interaction), Test of Spoken English as an optional supplement to Test of English as a Foreign Language (TOEFL-TSE), Spoken English Test held by Hong Kong Examinations Authority (HKEA-SET), Spoken English Test as a supplement to Test for English Majors (TEM-SET) in mainland China, and Spoken English Test as a supplement to College English Test (CET-SET). These tests are all held by recognized authorities at huge expenses. Finally, a large-scale oral test in Yarmouk University in Jordan (YU-SET) is discussed in the end, which is faced with a resource-lacking situation (such as that of budget) and of a program-specific nature similar to those facing us.

4.1 British SET: CUEFL-Oral Interaction

4.1.1 A brief description (Davies & West, 1989: 129-133)

Table 4.1 Introduction of test of Communicative Use of English as a Foreign Language (CUEFL)

Conducted by	University of Cambridge Local Examinations Syndicate (UCLES)/Royal Society of Arts Examinations Board (RSA)
Aims	The examinations are designed for non-native speakers who are living, working or studying in the UK, or intending to visit the country on a long- or short- term basis. They are also intended for candidates whose teaching has been 'communicative' but have no immediate plans to visit the UK. The aim is to measure whether or not the candidate can perform authentic tasks in English.

Level	At Basic, Intermediate and Advanced levels, four independent tests are offered: Reading, Listening, Writing and Oral Interaction. Candidates can choose any combination of these tests at any combination of levels (except that the same test may not be attempted at more than one level at each sitting).
Availability	The examinations are available through approved examination centers in the UK and overseas. Examinations are held twice a year, in late May and late November. No restriction in terms of age is imposed on entry, but the audience envisaged is 16+.
Results	Candidates are graded Pass or Fail for each test taken. Students must pass in both the Interview and Reading/Writing Tests to gain a certificate.

A description of CUEFL-Oral Interaction

The format of the test is the same at each level and lasts approximately 15 minutes. The test is divided into three parts, each observed by an assessor nominated by UCLES/RSA. Interactions are face-to-face.

Table 4.2 A description of CUEFL-Oral Interaction

Parts	Descriptions	Example from the Basic level
1	Interaction between the candidate and an interlocutor (normally a teacher known to the candidate)	A local club has invited you to give a talk to a group of visitors to the town or region where you live. Give them as much information as possible. You have asked a teacher to give you some ideas for your talk and you have been given the following suggestions. You may, of course, add some more of your own: ➤ Areas of natural beauty ➤ Climate ➤ Entertainment ➤ Shops ➤ Opportunities for sport ➤ Industry ➤ Local food ➤ Healthy facilities ➤ Local customs ➤ Education ➤ Housing In a few minutes, a teacher will ask you to tell him/her

		as much as you can about your hometown or region.
2	Interaction between candidates in pairs or threes without the interlocutor.	You and your partner are traveling in an air balloon. You each have a bag containing some valuable personal items (lists of contents supplied to candidates) but the pilot has told you that the balloon is too heavy and you must throw your bags out. You may, however, each keep two items. Find out from you partner what he/she has in his/her bag and discuss what items each of you wants to keep. Be prepared to give reasons for your choice.
3	Report from the candidates to the interlocutor on the interaction in Part 2.	

4.1.2 Comments

This test format combines the interview, learner-learner discussion and oral presentation techniques. The sequencing of part 2 and part 3 (oral presentation) is natural. However, there exist three problems:

1) The shift from part 1 (interview) to part 2 is disconnected in terms of topic. This is not consistent with the "student-centered thematic approach".

2) The interview format and the oral report to the interlocutor (the teacher) places the candidates at an inferior position. The candidates are not properly "centered".

3) The arrangement of having both an interlocutor and an assessor on the spot is impractical for our situation, in which the teacher resources are scant and no payment is available.

4.2 American SET: TOEFL-TSE

4.2.1 A brief description

Table 4.3 Introduction of Test of English as a Foreign Language (TOEFL)

(Davies & West, 1989: 21-25)

Conducted by	Educational Testing Service
Aims	To provide valid test scores indicating the English proficiency of non-native speakers seeking admission to colleges and universities in the United States and Canada. Also used in other countries by institutions where English is the medium of instruction. Each institution using TOEFL scores establishes its own acceptable range of scores. They are often used to place students in courses of the appropriate level of difficulty, or for determining whether additional study of English is required before an applicant can study successfully in English.
Level	TOEFL is designed for (US) grade 11 students and above.
Availability	Given only at centers established by the Education Testing Service, which are in approximately 170 countries and areas throughout the world. It is administered 12 times a year, once a month.
Results	Results are given as a score report, which is sent to the candidate and institutions named by the candidate. Current TOEFL score reports show the score on each of the three sections of the test (Listening comprehension, Structure and written expression, Vocabulary and reading comprehension) and the total score.

Table 4.4 A description of TOEFL-TSE

Conducted by	TSE Program Office
Aims	To evaluate the spoken English proficiency of non-native speakers who are graduates and must use spoken English extensively as teaching assistants, in seminars or in other academic contexts.
Level	Advanced level designed for those who need to use English fluently and confidently in an academic environment.
Availability	Administered at most TOEFL centers nine times a year. It is not part of the TOEFL test and a separate application form must be sent. TSE and TOEFL can usually be taken on the same day at most test centers.
Results	The test tapes are individually scored and the results show one overall score and three sub scores for (a) pronunciation (b) grammar and (c) fluency. The score report is sent directly to the candidate and to two institutions specified by the candidate.

Test type

Although it is easy to see that TOEFL-TSE is a typical indirect proficiency test adopting an analytical marking method, it is hard to judge whether it is criteria-referenced or norm-referenced. As a complement to TOEFL, TSE is intended to locate a candidate in the whole population of all candidates. So, theoretically it belongs to norm-referenced test type. However, in the process of assessment, neither are candidates randomly sampled, nor a norm is established to control the number of people of each level.

The content of TSE (Educational Testing Service, 1998:13-14)

The test takes approximately 30 minutes and the candidates' answers are recorded; no writing is required. The questions are either printed or recorded. The questions are divided into four sections:

1) Answer questions about themselves

2) Answer questions about a single picture

3) Construct a story from a series of pictures

4) Answer questions on general topics

Table 4.5 The contents of TOEFL-TSE

Parts	Descriptions	Examples
1	Answer questions about themselves	➤ What is the ID number on the cover of your test book? ➤ How long have you been studying English?
2	Answer questions about a single picture	The candidates are provided with a map of a city block and given 30 seconds for preparation. Then they are asked to answer questions, each question within 2 minutes. ➤ Choose one place on the map that you think I should visit and give me some reasons why you recommend this place. ➤ I'd like to see a movie. Please give me directions from the bus station to the movie theater. ➤ One of your favorite movies is playing at the theater. Please tell me about the movie and why you like it.
3	Construct a story from a series of pictures	Omitted
4	Answer questions on general topics	➤ Many people enjoy visiting zoos and seeing the animals. Other people believe that animals should not be taken from their natural surroundings and put into zoos. I'd like to know what you think about this issue. ➤ I'm not familiar with your field of study. Select a term used frequently in your field and define it for me.

4.2.2 Comments

TOEFL-TSE is a typical indirect (machine-mediated) test format. Thus it has all the advantages and disadvantages of an indirect SET (see 3.3.2).

Although this test type deserves research effort to compare it with direct SET, particularly in terms of reliability, validity, candidates' response, etc., it is not our favorite option due to its poor practicality. Some scholars do argue that indirect SET is practical in that a large number of candidates can be tested simultaneously by one examiner （e.g. 文秋芳, 1999: 71）. This is largely dependent on how the issue of practicality is understood. Indirect SET certainly is practical for candidates and for administration, but it is not necessarily practical for the assessment effort.

Let us use the concept of teacher time per student (TT/S) to find out its practicality. If the TOEFL-TSE format is used, then the TT/S would be around 40 minutes, which far exceeds acceptable amount of time for our SEAT, which is between 2.25 minutes and 4.5 minutes as discussed in 3.2.2).

Therefore, when it comes to assessment, TOEFL-TSE is even more time-consuming than interview, not to mention the dullness of both the candidates and the assessors who have to be faced with machines.

4.3 Hong Kong SET: HKEA-SET

4.3.1 A brief description

Hong Kong Examinations Authority (HKEA) annually conducts an SET as a component of English examinations for high school students. The test is held at two levels, one for grade five (equivalent to grade two of senior middle school in Mainland China) and one for grade seven (equivalent to college entrance examination in Mainland China). The SET for grade seven (hereafter referred to as HKEA-SET7) is discussed here since it is more adjacent in difficulty level to that of our SET.

In HKEA-SET7, four candidates are tested by two examiners/assessors within 20 minutes at one sitting. The test encompasses two sections: individual presentation and group discussion. The individual presentation lasts 8 minutes, each candidate being required to give a presentation of 2 minutes. Prior to the test, candidates are given a same passage and ten minutes for preparation. For a complete test paper, please refer to appendix 1.

4.3.2 Comments

This SET format combines the techniques of oral presentation and discussion.

Advantages

- It achieves high validity, authenticity, interactiveness, impact and practicality. To be specific, this test format can measure the linguistic competence not only at the sentence level, but also at discourse level (especially in the individual presentation section). Moreover, it also measures strategic competence adequately in the discussion section. Because of the cultural implications of the linguistic input, this SET format is able to facilitate in-depth thinking and production of language.

- It gets the examiners out of the chaos of administering the test. In this way, they can focus on assessment, which, in turn, improves reliability.

Limitations and possible improvement

- The individual presentation and group discussion are not very relevant in terms of the theme. To achieve coherence and fluent flow of the test procedure, the discussion task should preferably be designed on the basis of the individual presentation task.

- Using the same passage as linguistic input generates two problems. One is lack of information gap in the first part (individual presentation), which makes the communication dull. The other is that candidates may orally plagiarize others' presentation. A possible improvement might be supplying different passages to different candidates. Some people may argue that this practice might affect fairness of the test. But this danger could be avoided by making the linguistic comprehensible to the candidates in terms of both language and content. For example, a needs analysis can be done to survey candidates' knowledge structure, interest and linguistic level. Although this is very difficult for a test of general purposes, this is not so difficult for an achievement test, in which the examiners are the teachers of the candidates. Furthermore, candidates can be allowed to use dictionaries in case awkward keywords might hinder them from understanding the input.

- Although cross-cultural competence is tested to some degree on account of the cross-cultural nature of the linguistic input and the test task, this competence is not tested to the full. It the linguistic input could reveal the cultural differences between the different culture and the native culture of the candidates, cross-cultural competence would be better displayed in terms of sensitiveness, tolerance and flexibility (see 2.2 for discussion on cross-cultural competence).

4.4 Mainland China SET: TEM-SET

Since 1994, SET is conducted as a complement to the former Test for English Majors (TEM) band 4 in Mainland China in the form of indirect (machine-mediated) format. In 1997, the direct format was researched and is still under its trial stage (文秋芳, 1999). This format is similar to HKEA-SET7 (4.2). The only difference is that in HKEA-SET7, four candidates are tested at one sitting, while in TEM-SET direct format, two candidates are tested. Thus, for the descriptions and comments of this format, please refer to 4.2 on HKEA-SET7. In the following section only the indirect (machine-mediated) format is discussed.

4.4.1 A brief description

Task description

The oral test is designed for the second-year English majors. It involves different types of situations and a wide variety of topics. It consists of three tasks, each involving a particular speech activity.

Task One: Retell a story

The passage will be approximately 300 words long. It may be a story, accounts of experiences or anecdotes. The candidates have to start retelling immediately after they have heard the passage twice.

Task Two: Talk based on a given topic.

The given topic is very often related to the general theme of the passage candidates have heard previously. For example, the passage may describe someone's miserable life is his/her early childhood, and the topic the candidates are required to talk about is one happy incident in their childhood. After they have heard the given topic spoken on the test tape twice, they have three minutes to prepare their talk. Their talk is limited to three minutes.

Task Three: Role-play

The task involves two examinees. Each of them gets a sheet which contains a specific situation and a specified role he is expected to play. Although the situation is the same for the two examinees, their roles are different. For example, the given situation may be borrowing money. Student A wants to borrow 20 dollars from student B. Student A must try all the best to persuade Student B to lend him/her money while Student B must refuse A's request with politeness. Their preparation time is three minutes. Their conversation is limited to four minutes.

For a complete test paper of TEM-SET, please refer to appendix 2.

4.4.2 Comments

This test is claimed to have achieved high correlation to the written format of TEM, which is 0.59 before the norm-referenced transference of SET scores and 0.66 after the procedure. This transference is possible because the candidates are randomly sampled for each pair of assessors.

However, it suffers from all the limitations of an indirect (machine-mediated) test format (3.3.2). Although efforts has been made to make the communication real, for example, situations are provided for the role-play, the communication still appears inauthentic due to the setting of a language laboratory. Moreover, indirect SET does not necessarily reduces the cost and time, thus does not necessarily improve practicality in this sense (see 3.2.2 and 4.2.2 for more discussion on this issue).

The adoption of indirect SET format, according to 文秋芳 (1999: 101-103) was because of constraints of the real situation. TEM-SET is supposed to test all the English majors in China. If candidates are tested in several testing centers, as is done by most overseas SET, candidates have to take trains or buses to the centers. This seems impossible for now. But if teachers of colleges and universities are trained to be examiners/assessors, the assessment would be unreliable since these teachers would tend to give higher scores to students of their own colleges.

However, the SEAT in the present study does not have these practical constraints. This test is usually conducted within one college, so there is no necessity for the establishment of testing centers elsewhere. If the fear of teachers' being partial to their own students, they could switch their classes.

Another problem with the TEM-SET is that the role-play does not share the same topic with the first two test tasks. The shift of topic is not consistent with the thematic approach. In this sense, it has negative impact on teaching.

4.5 Mainland China SET: CET-SET

4.5.1 A brief description

CET-SET includes three parts (全国大学英语四、六级考试委员会, 1999: 1-20)

Table 4.6 Components of CET-SET

Parts	Time	Test tasks	Descriptions
I	5 min	Warming-up	Self-introduction: the candidates introduce themselves. Questions and answers: each candidates answers one question from the chief examiner
II	10 min	Individual presentations and group discussion	Individual presentations: after 1-minute preparation, each candidate gives a presentation of 1.5 minutes. Group discussion: the group discusses on a given topic.
III	5 min	Follow-up questions	Each candidate answers one more question to be confirmed of his or her oral competence.

For a sample test paper of CET-SET, please refer to appendix 3

4.5.2 Comments

In spite of the success in the trial stage (外语界, 1999: 58), the CET-SET format has some limitations for an achievement SET.

- The chief examiner dominates more than half of the test time. Therefore the sample of candidates' performance is relatively reduced to a small proportion of the test time. If the purpose of the test is to facilitate candidates' utterance rather than that of the tester, this would waste much of the valuable time of the testers, thus in this sense reduced practicality. Another limitation with this arrangement is that this is not in correspondence with the 'student-centered' approach to teaching, thus has negative impact on teaching. Finally, it increases the burden of the chief examiner, who is also an assessor, therefore reduces reliability.

- The picture stimuli have negative backwash effect (for discussion on this topic, please refer to 2.4, 2.5 and 3.4.7).

- The tasks are not authentic. First, the hierarchical social status difference between the examiner and the candidates is not the most frequent situation in candidates' real life. Second, the task does not feature the future situation in which candidates use spoken English. A brief needs analysis shows us that the most frequent use of spoken English for the Chinese college students will be with foreigners in conferences, seminars, working site cooperation, etc. In these cases, the mini-speech technique and questioning-answering techniques are the most important. Finally, it does not provide enough preparation time for the candidates. In the real situations, candidates often have some time before the talk to prepare on both the topics and the language.

- Cross-cultural competence is neglected in CET-SET. Because the topic of the discourse is not cross-cultural, this test is unlikely to reveal the sensitiveness, tolerance and flexibility of cross-cultural competence.

- CET-SET excludes candidates' sociolinguistic and strategic competence in the assessment criteria. Another even more serious danger is the neglect of content in the criteria. It is well known that the content is one major criterion in judging whether a piece of writing is good or not, as is shown in the assessment criteria of writing of CET (杨惠中 & Weir, 1998: 133-134). I would argue that there is no reason why content should be left out of the assessment criteria of SET since both SET and writing test try to measure productive skills. We certainly wouldn't assume that correct and fluent language alone would produce a good writer or a good speaker. A nonsense speaker certainly is not our aim of language teaching, even if he does not have errors in the speaking.

- It is mentioned above that the major conversation is between the examiners and the candidates. To be specific, it is usually the case that the examiners ask questions while the candidates answer. This adds to the tense atmosphere and creates possible affective filter/psychological tension.

- On the one hand, one or two speakers might dominate the talking in the discussion while the others are suppressed and kept silent. This is unfair to the less dominant ones. On the other, because the examiners are encouraged to let the candidate who performs best in the first part start the talking in the second (see CET Spoken English Test: Syllabus and Sample Test, page 7), the later ones might take advantage of the previous ones by adopting their ideas and language. This is unfair to the first speaker.

4.6 Jordan: YU-SET

4.6.1 A brief description

The YU-SET is conducted to test the two thousand students who pass through its one-year service English program. It was carried out to improve the overall accuracy of assessment and to produce a general motivational effect towards seriousness in learning of spoken English. It is strictly based on the syllabus and textbooks (a set readers in this case), thus is an achievement test in nature. However, it also serves for a diagnostic purpose.

The inclusion of this test format is because this is similar to our SET in three ways. First, it is a large-scale SEAT. Second, it is held by the classroom teachers rather than by a recognized testing authority. Third, it is administered within limitation of human resources similar to that facing us.

It takes the traditional form of interview in which one examiner acts as the interviewer while one candidate as the interviewee. The time of the interview is 8 minutes for each interviewee. It mainly includes two parts (Walker, 1990: 200-219). Part one is questions and answers on the set readers covered in the teaching program, and part two is conversation on a given topic. For a sample test paper of YU-SET, please refer to appendix 4.

This test was managed to measure two thousand students annually within limitation of human resources. Moreover, it paid considerable efforts to achieve inter-rater reliability, which is widely regarded as a potentially serious problem in oral tests. To be specific, in addition to measures taken in the preparation of the oral examination such as standardization of the interview format and evaluation criteria, training of testers, employment of moderators, etc, statistical analysis is conducted to compare testers' variations. A variety of statistical analytical tools were used, such as the one-way analysis of variance, multiple classification analysis and Student-Neuman-Keuls multiple comparison procedure, etc.

4.6.2 Comments

The YU-SET is a large success as a large-scale achievement test. However, it has some limitations against the situation in the present study.

- It has all the limitations of traditional interviews (see 3.4.5)

- Although it is practical in the case of Yarmouth University, it is still considered as consuming too much human resources. The consumption of teacher time per student TT/S in this test was 8 minutes, which exceeds our acceptable amount of TT/S of 2.25-4.5 minutes.

- The statistical analysis for the control of inter-rater reliability is based on random sampling of candidates. However this is considered for now too troublesome since this would add burden to administration. Presumably, our SEAT should be conducted when candidates would normally have had their English classes.

But is this statistical analysis necessary? The necessity depends on how the test result is interpreted and used. In the case of Yarmouth University, the result of the SET is used to determine whether the candidates are allowed to receive the English medium instruction provided by the university. Therefore, inter-rater reliability is taken very seriously. Statistical analysis achieved this purpose. It detected two testers out of twenty one might have produced unreliable scores and fourteen out of two thousand students might have passed the test while they had been failed. These students, therefore, might be retested or their scores simply adjusted upwards to a pass grade.

However, this statistical effort is considered not so essential for our purpose. On the one hand, the result of our SEAT would not be used for such serious purposes as to determine whether students can further their education. The major purpose of our test is for the impact on teaching. On the other hand, even if statistical analysis is conducted, regardless of the administration and statistical cost it might add to the test, seriously mistreated candidates occupy such a small percentage of the whole population (in the YU-SET, the percentage was 0.7%) that this small percentage could be neglected in our test.

Nevertheless, an important implication could be drawn from the practice of YU-SET, i.e., one-assessor model for a subjective test of spoken English could still achieve acceptable reliability. Although this one-assessor model has been prevalent in the testing of writing, it is not so widespread in the testing of speaking. Among the six SET discussed in this chapter, only CUEFL-Oral Interaction and YU-SET adopted the one-assessor model (in CUEFL-Oral Interaction, another teacher is also present as the interlocutor), while the other four tests used two-assessor model.

This implication is valuable for our test because the one-assessor model, if applicable, could reduce the TT/S by half, thus considerably improves practicality.

4.7 A summary of this chapter

The contrastive study of six SEAT formats is summarized in table 4.7.

Table 4.7 Differences of the six SET formats and possible improvements for our SEAT design

SET formats	Test types	Techniques used	Number of assessors	TT/S	Comments and possible improvements
CUEFL-Oral Interaction	Direct criteria-referenced proficiency test adopting analytical marking	Interview Role-play Oral report	One assessor with an interlocut or present	10-15 min	➢ In order to achieve practicality, the interlocutor could be omitted, leaving the interaction be among candidates. ➢ Different test tasks should preferably be on the same theme.
TOEFL-TSE	Indirect proficiency test adopting analytical marking (reference to norm or criteria unknown)	Questions and answers Using pictures	Two assessors	40 min	➢ Indirect SET is not practical in terms of TT/S. ➢ If this format is adopted, one-assessor model can improve practicality.
HKEA-SET7	Direct norm-referenced proficiency test adopting analytical marking	Oral presentation, candidate-candidate discussion	Two assessors	10 min	➢ The individual presentation and discussion should preferably be based on one topic. ➢ Each candidate should be provided with a different passage on one cross-cultural theme.
TEM-SET	Indirect norm-referenced proficiency test adopting analytical marking	Story-retelling based on aural input, Monologue on a given topic Role-play with another candidate	Two assessors	40 min	➢ Indirect SET is not necessarily practical in terms of TT/S. ➢ If this format is adopted, one-assessor model can improve practicality, and different test tasks should preferably be on the same theme.
CET-SET	Direct criteria-referenced proficiency test adopting analytically-holistic marking	Questions and answers Oral presentation, discussion	Two assessors, one of which plays the role of the interlocut or	10 min	➢ The role of the interlocutor can be excluded. ➢ Linguistic input on a cross-cultural theme is preferable to pictures. ➢ Sociolinguistic and strategic competence should be revealed in the assessment criteria.
YU-SET	Direct criteria-referenced achievement test adopting analytical marking	Interview	One assessor	8 min	➢ One-assessor model for a subjective test of spoken English could still achieve acceptable reliability. ➢ Higher practicality can be achieved if the interview is replaced by multi-candidate activities.

The above contrastive study of eight representative SET formats has the following implications for the SEAT design in the present study:

1) A SET can employ two or more techniques and sequence them properly in order to make a "useful" test.

2) The one-assessor model without an interlocutor may greatly reduce teacher time per student (TT/S), thus improves practicality.

3) Indirect SET actually consumes more TT/S, thus is impractical for an SEAT.

4) Considerable effort has to be made to construct a practical SEAT in the present study. Besides adoption of one-assessor model, an SEAT can employ the techniques which is capable of testing a group of candidates together at one sitting.

Part two: Empirical research

After an exploration into theories relevant to the practice of the SEAT, we have got implications for SEAT design and execution. In the light of these theories and their implications, we are finally able to construct and execute our SEAT, thus to forward into the part of empirical research. The empirical research here is conducted at two phases. In phase one study, four SEAT formats will be empirically tried out. Based on the result of phase one study, we will carry out an in-depth study, i.e., we will develop a presentation and discussion (P&D) format, conduct it and evaluate it in a thorough manner.

Chapter 5 Phase one study: Four SEAT formats

This chapter discusses a research project on four SEAT formats for Chinese non-English majors. Three formats are discussed first because they are conducted on the same subjects. Later, the fourth format is dealt with separately because it is conducted on another group of subjects. The four research projects make up a project done by me together with three other student researchers as term papers for a course of language testing taught by Professor Shao Yongzhen as part of the requirements for MA degree program of Linguistics and Applied Linguistics in Zhejiang University.

5.1 A contrastive study of three SEAT formats

The three SEAT formats are all conducted on 37 sophomores of a class majoring in Computer Software Development of grade 98 in Hangzhou Institute of Electronics Engineering in January 2000.

5.1.1 Introduction

The following contrastive study of three SEAT formats, namely mini-speech, role-play and machine-mediated SET, tries to answer the following questions:

1) Which rating method is more reliable, analytical or holistic rating?

2) How is the inter-rater reliability of an SEAT?

3) How are the different criteria related to one another?

4) What strategies are revealed in the three formats? Which of them are contributory? Which are noncontributory?

5) What topics do Chinese college English learners favor in an SEAT?

6) What comments do candidates have on the three SEAT formats?

7) What are the differences among the three SEAT formats in terms of practicality and concurrent validity?

5.1.2 Methodology

5.1.2.2 Specifications of the three SEAT formats

Test 1: Mini-speech

Test content

In the mini-speech format, four candidates are tested at one sitting. Each candidate has to complete two tasks.

Table 5.1 Test tasks each candidate completes in the mini-speech SEAT format

Parts	Descriptions
1. mini-speech (2 min)	The mini-speech should include at least three parts8.
	1. **Introduction:** This may include greetings, self-introduction, introduction of the topic to arouse the interest of the audience, presentation of key words and new vocabulary, etc.
	2. **Main body:** This sub-section will give the main points and the details, whether they are narrative, argumentative, expository or descriptive, or a combination of more than one style of speaking.
	3. **Conclusion:** Here, the speaker will summarize his speech in a powerful, impressive, or inspirational way.
	In the course of the whole speech, the audience (the other candidates) is required to take notes, give appropriate response (facial expression or nodding of the head, for example) to the speech.
2. Questions and answers (2 min)	This part will be composed of two sub-sections.
	1. Short questions and answers for the comprehension of the speech. Here the speaker may invite questions on the understanding of his speech, and the audience will ask for clarification of the main idea or the details.
	2. Short questions and answers for the ideas of the audience. Here the speaker will invite the comments of the audience on his topic, and the audience may present their own similar experience, ideas or proposals.

Test administration

---

[8] The three parts of the speech is decided on the basis of a speech training course for international students, Speech Communication for International Students, edited by Dale and Wolf (1988).

Two examiners test four candidates at one sitting. Both examiners give marks, meanwhile one of them ensures the procedure. The procedure goes according to the following flow chart.

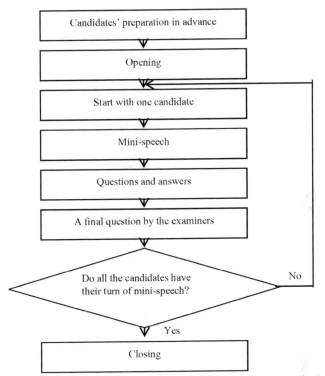

Figure 5.1 The procedural flow chart of mini-speech SET format

In the mini-speech, candidates choose what to talk about after they are informed of the test format and requirements a week before the test. The topic chosen has to be of general interest, controversial, centered around students' study and social lives and comprehensible without special technical knowledge. The speech can be narrative, argumentative, descriptive, expository or a combination of different styles. Cross-cultural topics are preferred.

Rating method

In order to analyze the differences between analytical and holistic rating methods, examiners give scores by both methods. But they are not allowed to compare their scores or reach a holistic score by adding up their analytical scores. They are trained in advance by rating a sample group of candidates.

The criteria for assessment will be applied not only to the speeches given, but also to the questions and answers between the speaker and the audience.

- Content (Components of the speech complete, main ideas standing out and details substantive)

- Accuracy (Correct use of pronunciation, vocabulary and structure)

- Range (A wide range of vocabulary and structure)

- Fluency (Appropriate speed, stress and intonation)

- Discourse management (Cohesion and coherence)

- Register or appropriacy (Use of language appropriate to context, function and intention)

- Strategy (Effective use of linguistic and non-linguistic strategies)

- Participation (The audience's ability to ask questions and to present his own ideas on the speeches during each seminar session)

To make the rating scale easier, the assessment criteria are arranged into four groups and each group is given equal weighting. However, a different weighting of the above mentioned assessment criteria can be used according to different testing situations.

Table 5.2 Rating scales of the mini-speech SEAT

Scores	Content	Accuracy and range	Fluency and discourse management	Register, strategy and participation
22-25 Excellent	➢ Components of the speech complete ➢ Main ideas standing out ➢ Details substantive	➢ Correct pronunciation ➢ Correct use of vocabulary and structure ➢ A wide range of vocabulary and structure	➢ Appropriate speed, stress and intonation ➢ Effective use of cohesive devices ➢ Coherence achieved	➢ Use of language appropriate to context, function and intention ➢ Effective use of linguistic and non-linguistic strategies ➢ The audience's ability to ask questions and to present his own ideas during seminar session
19-21 Good	➢ Lack of necessary components in the subsections of the speech ➢ Main ideas stated but not very powerful ➢ Details stated but not enough	➢ Containing a few pronunciation errors ➢ Containing a few errors in vocabulary and structure ➢ A basically satisfactory range of vocabulary and structure to deal with the topic	➢ A little hasty or slow, some wrong stress or intonation ➢ Acceptable use of cohesive devices ➢ Satisfactory logic and coherence	➢ Containing some language too formal or too casual ➢ Satisfactory use of linguistic and non-linguistic strategies ➢ Having some difficulty asking questions and presenting ideas
15-18 Acceptable	➢ Lacking a major subsection in the speech ➢ Main ideas not clear ➢ Some details irrelevant	➢ Errors of pronunciation affecting communication ➢ Errors of vocabulary and communication affecting communication ➢ A minimum range of vocabulary and structure	➢ Inappropriate speed, wrong stress or intonation affecting communication ➢ Occasional or wrong use of cohesive devices ➢ Cohesion not well achieved	➢ Register of language affecting communication ➢ Occasional or some wrong use of strategies ➢ Questions and ideas irrelevant
Below 15 Poor or failure	➢ Subsections not obvious ➢ Main ideas not stated ➢ Most details irrelevant or no supporting details	➢ Full of errors on pronunciation ➢ Full of errors on vocabulary and structure ➢ Vocabulary and structure scarce or repetitive	➢ Inability to control speed, full of stress and intonation errors ➢ No use of cohesive devices ➢ Very bad coherence	➢ Register of language cause inability of communication ➢ No or totally wrong use of strategies ➢ Unable to present questions and one's own ideas

Table 5.3 Score description of the mini-speech SEAT

87-100	Excellent
74-86	Good
60-73	Acceptable
Below 60	Poor or failure

Test 2: Role-play

Test content

A journalist of a newspaper wants to make a report on the problem of enlarging the enrollment of universities. He or she will interview three persons. One is a middle school student who is preparing for the entrance examination of universities; one is a common student of our college; the third is a college teacher. Then the journalist will give his or her report to the newspaper.

Role-cards:

Role 1:

You're a journalist and you want to make a report about the problem of enlarging the enrollment of universities (高校扩大招生规模). So you'll interview three persons. One is a middle school student who is preparing for the entrance examination of universities, one is a common student of our college, and the third is a college teacher. You must prepare some questions for your interview. After the interview, you have to give the oral report to all of us.

Role 2:

You're a common student who is preparing for the entrance examination of universities. A journalist wants to interview you about the problem of enlarging the enrollment of universities (高校扩大招生规模). Please give your opinion of it.

Role 3:

You're a common student of our college. A journalist wants to interview you about the problem of enlarging the enrollment of universities (高校扩招问题). Please give your opinion of it.

Role 4:

You're a college teacher. A journalist wants to interview you about the problem of enlarging the enrollment of universities (高校扩招问题). You're worried about the qualities of the students after enlarging the enrollment. Please give your opinion to the journalist.

Test administration

The test is conducted in the following procedure at one sitting, each sitting lasting 12 minutes.

1) One examiner briefly introduces the topic to four candidates in English.

2) The examiners assign different role-cards to the candidates.

3) The candidates have three minutes to prepare. Communication among candidates is not allowed during this period.

4) The candidates play their roles one by one. Each candidate is required to talk in a time-scale from one to three minutes.

5) The examiners give marks independently in the process of the role-play or after the examinees leave. But no discussion is allowed between them in the process of marking.

Rating method

The assessment criteria of the oral test include:

Table 5.4 Assessment criteria for the role-play SEAT

Criteria	Marks
Accuracy	2 points
Fluency	2 points
Size	2 points
Flexibility	2 points
Discourse management	2 points
Total	10 points

Test 3: The Machine-mediated SEAT

Test content

Table 5.5 A sample test paper for the machine-mediated SEAT

Test tasks	Content	Time	Score weighting
Self-introduction		1 min	15
Picture description and story telling	A series of cartoon pictures named "father" describing a story	6 min	35
Verbal essay	The person I respect the most	3 min	25
Questions for long answers	Should TV commercials be banned? Why or why not?	2 min	25
Total		12 min	100

Test administration

The instructions of the test are recorded on a tape. The candidates are given a test paper, on which the test instructions and the pictures are printed. The whole test is conducted in a language laboratory. Each candidate records his or her utterances on the tape for later assessment.

Rating method

The assessor is required to give both holistic and analytical scores. Score weighting for analytical rating is specified in table 5.5.

Table 5.6 Assessment criteria for the machine-mediated SEAT

	Expressiveness	Accuracy	Fluency	Size	Content
16-20					
11-15					
6-10					
0-5					

Expressiveness: the intelligibility of the candidate's talk, regardless of grammatical mistakes

Accuracy and fluency: the candidate's performance

Size: the length of the candidate's contribution, and the complexity of his sentences

Content: whether the candidate's contribution is relevant to the task specified

5.1.2.3 Data analysis methods

Three methods are adopted for the research. They are statistical analysis of test scores, questionnaire for the candidates and interview of examiners. In order to justify the concurrent validity of the SEAT, the candidates' scores on their written final examination held a week after the SEAT and the teachers' subjective assessments of the candidates' oral proficiency are also collected.

5.1.3 Results and discussions

Question 1. Which rating method is more reliable, analytical or holistic rating?

In order to find out the differences between analytical and holistic rating, I did a paired sample T-test for the mini-speech format. The result is shown in table 5.7.

Table 5.7 T-test for paired samples of scores by analytical and holistic ratings (mini-speech)

	Analytical	Holistic
Mean	74.82432	74.14865
Variance	80.19745	82.42868
Pairs	37	37
Correlation	0.982908	
SE of means	0	
Df(Degree of freedom)	36	
t_s (Statistical t-value)	2.458521	
P(T<=t) one-tailed sig	0.009447	
t_α(one-tailed limit)	1.688297	
P(T<=t) two-tailed sig	0.018894	
t_α(two-tailed limit)	2.028091	

(Significant at $\alpha = 0.05$)

From the above table, we can see that the correlation between the two rating methods is 0.982 and that the statistical t-value t_s is 2.459, which is higher than the one-tailed limit t_α(1.669). This means although the two rating methods reveal high correlation, we are still able to deny the no difference hypothesis between them.

In order to find out which rating method is more reliable, I calculated the correlations between SET scores and the students' scores in their final examination and the teacher's assessment of students' oral skills, which is shown as follows.

Table 5.8 Correlations of SE scores and other variants (mini-speech)

	Analytical	Holistic	Final	Teacher's assessment
Analytical	1			
Holistic	0.983	1		
Final	**0.524**	**0.519**	1	
Teacher's assessment	0.615	0.615	0.743	1

From table 5.8, we may find that the analytical scores tend to relate more to the results of the final examination. Therefore, a conclusion may be drawn that analytical rating may be more desirable, especially when the test is also used for a diagnostic purpose.

Question 2. How is the inter-rater reliability?

In the mini-speech SET, each candidate is scored by two assessors in order for the researchers to find out the inter-rater reliability. Because four candidates are scored by all the assessors at the examiner training stage prior to the SEAT, only 33 candidates' scores are calculated.

Table 5.9 Inter-rater reliability between two groups of assessors

Assessor group	Mean	SD	Candidate number	Median	Max	Min
Group 1	73.79	8.78	33	73	93	57
Group 2	75.58	7.54	33	76	92	60
Difference	1.79	1.24	0	3	1	3

From table 5.9, it can be concluded that the scores of the candidates given by the two groups of assessors reveal no significant differences. The mean difference is only 1.79 and the standard deviation difference is only 1.24.

The implication of this conclusion is that in the case of lack of human resources, the one-assessor model can be employed, provided that adequate training and supervision are available to the assessors.

Question 3. How are the different criteria related to one another?

The correlations among different criteria and those between each criterion and overall oral proficiency are calculated in the mini-speech SEAT (see table 5.10).

Table 5.10 Correlations among different assessment criteria and that between them and total of analytical scores (mini-speech)

	Content	Accuracy & range	Fluency & discourse	Register, strategy & participation	Total scores
Content	8				
Accuracy & range	0.763287	1			
Fluency & discourse	0.774833	0.9121287	1		
Register, strategy & participation	0.768351	0.8185342	0.879238	1	
Total scores	0.883699	0.9364532	0.961799	0.936625	1

Table 5.10 illustrates that, although all the analytical scores are very closely related to total scores, there are still differences of correlations.

1. Content does not relate so closely to other variants as the other criteria. The same is true with variant 4. This indicates the necessity of including content and meta-linguistic factors as part of assessment criteria for communicative SET.

2. Accuracy and fluency are very closely related. This implies that, as both variants constitute linguistic competence, they could be merged into one single criterion, which could be properly termed as "language". Thus, the above seemingly over-complicated rating scales could be simplified into three sub-categories, namely, "content", "language" and "meta-linguistic factors".

3. The criterion most related to the total score is fluency. This shows that fluency is the most important elements in oral skills. The implication of this finding is that biggest efforts should be made to train learners' fluency if we want them to get high oral proficiency.

Question 4. What strategies are revealed in the three formats? Which of them are contributory? Which are noncontributory?

In the questionnaire (see appendix 5), in order to investigate into the strategic use of candidates, eleven strategies are listed by referring to the previous studies on learner strategies, among which eight are recognized as contributory and three as non-contributory (see Ellis & Sinclair, 1989; O'Malley & Chamot, 1990; Oxford, 1990; Rubin, 1975; 秦晓晴, 1998; 文秋芳, 1996; 吴一安，刘润清，1993; Cohen, 1998.etc). The candidates are required to choose strategies they have employed in the three SEAT formats. The results are as follows.

Table 5.11 Number of candidates using strategies in the three SEAT formats

Item	Strategy	Contributory or not	Mini-speech	Role-play	Machine-mediated SEAT
A	Mental outlining before speaking	Yes	37	15	21
B	Proper opening remarks with a sketch of the speech	Yes	4	0	2
C	Thinking in English	Yes	3	3	9
E	Eliciting by synonymy, repetition and paraphrasing	Yes	8	6	7
F	Employing facial and body language	Yes	9	9	0
H	Using language uttered by other speakers	Yes	1	5	1
J	Tolerating of minor incomprehension for the smooth flow of communication	Yes	14	16	0
K	Polite interruption and request for repetition	Yes	4	11	0
D	Always thinking in Chinese and translating	No	3	15	17
G	Neglecting the audience	No	9	4	2
I	Focusing on some specific words rather than the main ideas while listening	No	8	7	1

Table 5.12 A summary of contributory and noncontributory strategies candidates used in the three formats

Strategies	Mini-speech		Role-play		Machine-mediated SEAT	
Contributory	80	80.0%	65	71.4%	40	66.7%
Noncontributory	20	20.0%	26	28.6%	20	33.3%
Total	100	100%	91	100%	60	100%

From the above table, we can see that in the mini-speech format, more candidates have employed strategies and a majority of the strategies they employ are contributory. In the machine-mediated SEAT, fewer candidates use strategies and about one third of these strategies are noncontributory.

This result indicates that the mini-speech SEAT better reveals the strategic competence of the candidates than the other two formats. Consequently, mini-speech is more desirable for the positive impact on teaching of spoken English in terms of strategic development.

Question 5. What topics do Chinese college English learners favor?

The topics used by the candidates in the mini-speech SEAT are grouped into nine categories by means of a "key-word analysis". They are presented as follows.

Table 5.13 Topics selected by candidates in the mini-speech SET

Type	Sub-type	Number	Total
College study	Methodology	1	5
	Examination system	2	
	English learning	1	
	Plagiarism	1	
Entertainment	Hobby and interest	2	3
	Music and Movie	1	
Sports	Basketball	2	4
	Football	1	
	Famous athletes	1	
Background	Family	1	3
	Hometown	1	
	City life and country life	1	
Science and technology	Internet	2	5
	Software	1	
	Creation and invention	1	
	Uses of salt	1	
Fashions	Private cars	1	4
	Part-time jobs	3	
Human relationship	Children and parents	1	3
	Man-woman relationship	2	
Personality	Traits leading to success	1	2
	Independence	1	
Others	Fresh water	1	7

	Festival-Christmas	1	
	How to keep healthy	1	
	Famous people	1	
	Opening-up and reform	1	
	Patriotism	1	
	War and peace	1	
Sum			36

I bothered to study the topics for two purposes. One is for further design of the SEAT; the other is for spoken English teaching. The table above may serve as a needs analysis for both purposes. On the one hand, when designing the SET with a given topic, we ought to know what topics the candidates are familiar with and are willing to talk about. On the other hand, these topics can be a reference for teachers to formulate their teaching plan of spoken English.

Question 6. What comments do candidates have on the three SEAT formats?

Table 5.14 Candidates' assessment of the three SEAT formats

SET format	Assessment	Number	Percentage
	a. Very good	4	11%
	b. Good	25	68%
Mini-speech	c. Average	8	22%
	d. Bad	0	0%
	e. Very bad	0	0%
	a. Very good	11	30%
	b. Good	15	41%
Role-play	c. Average	11	30%
	d. Bad	0	0%
	e. Very bad	0	0%
	a. Very good	2	5%
	b. Good	12	32%
Machine-recorded test	c. Average	19	51%
	d. Bad	4	11%
	e. Very bad	0	0%

Table 5.14 shows that the candidates favor the mini-speech the most since the majority of them (79%) accepted the mini-speech SET format as a good one. This percentage is the highest among those on the other two formats, which are 71% and 37% respectively. None of them regards mini-speech as a bad format.

Comments from candidates on the mini-speech format are analyzed and listed as follows for the benefit of improving the three SEAT formats in the future.

Table 5.15 Major comments from candidates on mini-speech SET format

		Comments	Qualities concerned	Number	Percentage
Advantages	➢	Able to avoid the dilemma of having nothing to say in other SET formats	Reliability, validity	16	44%
	➢	Adequate time to display one's overall oral proficiency	Reliability, validity, practicality	8	22%
	➢	Able to test logical utterance	Validity, authenticity, impact	5	14%
	➢	Low affective filter	Reliability	6	16%
Disadvantages	➢	Unable to test flexible ability to deal with unexpected situations	Validity, interactiveness, authenticity	12	32%

Table 5.16 Major comments from candidates on role-play SET format

		Comments	Qualities concerned	Number	Percentage
Advantages	➢	Able to test flexible use of language	Validity, interactiveness, authenticity, impact	33	89%
Disadvantages	➢	More challenging than the other two formats	Reliability	12	32%
	➢	Difficult to understand speakers of poor oral competence	Reliability	9	24%

Table 5.17 Major comments from candidates on machine-mediated SET format

	Comments		Qualities concerned	Number	Percentage
Advantages	➢	Objective	Reliability	9	24%
	➢	Relaxed atmosphere in the absence of the interviewer	Reliability	13	35%
Disadvantages	➢	Lacking of authentic situation of language use	Validity, authenticity, impact	17	46%
	➢	Rigid and dull procedure	Validity, authenticity, impact	8	22%

Question 7. What are the differences among the three SEAT formats in terms of practicality and concurrent validity?

Suppose the one-rater approach was adopted, the practicality of the three SET formats could be calculated in terms of the teacher time per candidate, the result of which is shown in table 5.18. This table also shows the correlations of the three formats to the mid-term examination.

Table 5.18 The TT/S and correlation of the three SEAT formats

	mini-speech	role-play	machine-mediated SEAT
TT/S	4 min	3 min	12 min
Correlation to mid-term examination	0.519	0.396	0.738

From table 5.18, we can see that the machine-mediated SEAT is more related to the written test of English, thus has achieved high concurrent validity. But it is also the most time-consuming in terms of assessment. The role-play is the most practical, but has the lowest correlation to the written test, thus its reliability is under doubt. The mini-speech is a little less practical. But it can also be time-efficient if administered properly. Meanwhile, it achieves the acceptable correlation to the written test of English. The machine-mediated SEAT has the highest correlation to the written test of English, but it is not practical for an SEAT.

5.2 An empirical study of the discussion and presentation (D&P) SEAT format

5.2.1 Introduction

The D&P SEAT format encompasses a discussion and an oral presentation. The table below compares discussion and oral presentation in different aspects.

Table 5.19 A comparison of discussion and oral presentation (CHEN, 2000: 5)

	Discussion	*Oral presentation*
TLU(target language use)	More common; ranging from family discussion to Board meeting and political discussion	Less common; including oral report, giving a lecture; giving a running speech; giving a press conference, etc.
Participation	all participants have equal chance to contribute to, carry on or shift the topic; interlocutors feel free to interrupt, express different ideas or ask for clarification	One speaker in most of the time; audience have little freedom to intervene
Turn length	Short speaking turns; interactive exchanges; requiring one or two utterances at one time	Extended speaking turns
Conditions	Usually improvised; proceeding under time constraints	Usually prepared; allowing a planning stage
Style of output	Informal discourses; fragmentary utterances, frequent repetition and overlaps are acceptable	a well contrived oral presentation requires a neat discourse organization and development of ideas and themes
Major speaking skills involved	Interaction-based; two-way communication; testing interaction routines, negotiation skills, negotiation of meaning, management of interaction agenda management, and turn taking	One-way communication; testing informational routines

David Nunan (1993: 32) gives a list of qualities a successful speaker should be endowed with, including

- …
- transactional and interpersonal skills
- skills in taking short and long speaking turns
- skills in the management of interaction
- skills in negotiating meaning;
- skills in knowing about and negotiating purposes for conversations
- using appropriate conversational formulae and fillers.

After comparing the two test types, the researcher believes that theoretically, discussion and oral presentation can complement each other in attaining an overall perspective of a learner's oral competence (CHEN, 2000: 6)

5.2.2 Methodology

Subjects

The subjects in this study were 45 first-year students (9 females and 36 males) in Zhejiang University at the end of their first term of college English language study. Shortly after the oral test, they took the final examination.

Test content (Topic)

In devising the topics, the researcher maintains the following principles. The topics should be

- relative to learners' life;

- controversial;

- problem-solving or decision-making;

- project-based;

The principles are formulated to ensure that the tasks and topics won't cause much stress on the part of test-takers and will elicit their optimal performance in the test (CHEN, 2000: 8).

Test administration

48 candidates are divided into 8 groups, each group including 6

members. 4 groups are tested at the same time. Five classrooms were occupied to conduct the test (one discussion room and the other four both as waiting rooms and for the assessment of oral presentation session). A team of six examiners took part in this administration. Two of them would assess learner performance in discussion and each of the others stays in a waiting room, conducting, assessing and tape-recording oral presentation.

When the test begins, one member in every group is randomly chosen to go to the discussion room. Meanwhile, the five other group members are in the waiting room. In designing each of the tasks, the researcher prepares two sets of roles, one set for the oral reporters, one set for the audience.

Table 5.20 Roles assigned to candidates in the D&P SEAT

Task	Title	Roles for candidates /reporters	Roles for audience
1	Travel Planning	Organizers of classroom excursion	The other students in the class
2	A Problem Page	Freshmen in Zhijiang College of Zhejiang University	Worried Parents who want to know something about college life in Zhijiang College
3	Donatio n	Members in Students' Union	Students and important people in college
4	Part-tim e Jobs	Members in Students' Union	Students and important people in college
5	Examina tion or not	Members in Students' Union	Principals of some top universities and famous educators
6	A Mock Election	Organizers and runners	Voters
7	A Family Problem	Neighbors	The family in trouble

Take Item 1 as an example. While the test-takers are arguing whose hometown the class should visit and how to arrange the excursion in the discussion room, the others would be discussing what kind of places they would like to visit. When the discussion ended and the candidates had made their decision, the audience had also arrived at a list of questions they concerned about the travel arrangement. Thus they had created an expectation for what the report would be about. During the report, they could check whether the travel plan lived up to their expectation or not. If some of the questions in their list were not covered in oral presentation yet, they might well ask the reporter (CHEN, 2000: 8).

Rating method

Both holistic and analytic approaches are employed because the researcher believes that holistic rating is high in validity while analytic rating is high in reliability so that they can complement each other. In holistic scoring, the assessor's judgment was based on his general impression of the speaker's overall speaking competence. The analytic marking was based on the rating scales. Considering the differences between discussion and oral presentation and the sub-skills involved, in this test, the researcher designed two rating scales. In joint discussion, the testers assessed the test-takers' performance in terms of accuracy, fluency, comprehensibility and strategy and appropriateness in the process of interaction. In presentation, the testers assessed them in terms of accuracy, fluency, comprehensibility and discourse management. The analytic ratings were then totaled and the resultant scores were compared with the outcome of holistic rating (CHEN, 2000: 9).

5.2.3 Results and Discussion

To judge its validity and reliability, the researcher makes reference to the final examination in early January 2000, which are administered to the same set of candidates a week later (see table 5.21).

Table 5.21 Results of the D&P SEAT and coefficients between the SEAT and the final examination (CHEN, 2000: 9)

		DISCUSSION	PRESENTATION	AVERAGE	FINAL
MEAN SCORE		69.111	71.344	70.211	69.556
SD		11.134	9.7854	8.9589	5.7483
COEFFI.	Discussion	—	0.6673	0.9236	**0.3958**
	PRESENTATION		—	0.9018	**0.5332**
	AVERAGE			—	**0.5128**
	FINAL				—

From the table 5.21, it is observed that the validity coefficient between the average score of the D&P SEAT (Aver.) and the final examination is 0.51. This indicates that the D&P SEAT format is reliable and valid (CHEN, 2000: 10).

The table also reveals that the presentation bears a higher correlation to the final examination than the discussion. In addition, the average score for presentation is higher than that for discussion. Besides, its standard deviation is smaller than that in discussion. All these outcomes are a little surprising for in designing the test because the researcher had expected that the discussion session would be more relaxing and learners tend to perform better while presentation was more demanding, therefore it should be more difficult and capable to distinguish the speakers (CHEN, 2000: 11).

To settle her doubts, the researcher interviewed some students, including top students, intermediate students as well as poor ones. Almost unanimously, they held that presentation part was easier. From their responses and my analysis of the procedure, the researcher justifies their claim as follows:

1) The most important reason is that time was limited for discussion part. Four candidates have to share the 10 minutes. Besides, they had to read the topics, some of which were quite long, and they had little planning time for what they were going to say. Although the oral presentation also lasts 10 minutes, the reporter dominates most of this time. The oral presentation is also more reassuring because the reporter is allowed some planning time to prepare their report and even entitled to read their notes as a reminder. In this sense, oral presentation session has priority over discussion.

2) Another reason lies in the audience and the setting of the examination rooms. The first session (the discussion) is held in teacher's office. The short distance between the assessors and the test-takers made the atmosphere quite threatening. On the contrary, the oral presentation was held in ordinary classrooms, which might be more comfortable to the reporters.

3) Because in the discussion, four students were assessed simultaneously, it would be easy to make comparison between their performances. The inferiority or superiority tended to be exaggerated, which may have led to the result that the standard deviation for discussion was larger (CHEN, 2000: 11).

5.3 A summary of this chapter

The empirical research project on four SET formats discussed in this chapter provides valuable insights into SET construction and administration. These insights could be summarized as follows:

1) There are differences between analytical and holistic rating methods. The former seems to be a little more related to overall linguistic proficiency revealed in written test of English.

2) Adequate training of experienced teachers as assessors of SET could yield desirable inter-rater reliability. Therefore, in the case of lacking human resources, the one-rater model could be used.

3) The assessment criteria of SET could include three elements, namely, content, language and meta-linguistic competence.

4) The mini-speech format, which is actually a combination of oral presentation and discussion, seems to facilitate more contributory strategies than the role-play and the machine mediated SEAT. Thus, combination of presentation and discussion may be a desired format for testing strategic competence and for positive impact on learning.

5) The topics chosen by candidates in mini-speech can be used as a reference on themes for further SET development.

6) Candidates favor the mini-speech more than the role-play and machine-mediated SEAT. Their comments are also valuable for the development of SET.

7) Although the machine-mediated SET achieves higher concurrent validity, it is not so practical for an SEAT because the assessment consumes too much time.

8) Oral presentation, in which the candidates are provided with time for preparation, seems has a priority over discussion in that the former has higher correlation to overall proficiency revealed in written test of English.

However, this project, which was conducted for the writing of a course paper prior to the undertaking of this degree paper, has four limitations judging from the literature review on theories on speaking and SET.

1) Cross-cultural competence is neglected. To be specific, the topics chosen in the tasks are not cross-cultural.

2) There is no sufficient linguistic input to provide enough information and language needed for the generation of oral production.

3) The tasks are not centered on one theme in the mini-speech. Because each candidate chooses his own topic, several different topics exist at one sitting. This increases the difficulty of processing of language, thus add up to the difficulty of discussion. Moreover, the swift shift of topics irrelevant to each other is unnatural and inauthentic.

4) The proposed "discussion and presentation" SEAT format is not practical because the procedure is too complicated, and because it consumes too many resources. For example, it requires many separate rooms and many examiners/assessors as well. Besides, in the D&P format, the time allocation of the discussion and presentation is not so appropriate because four candidates have to share 10 minutes in the discussion but one candidate owns 10 minutes for the presentation.

Chapter 6 Phase two study: "presentation and discussion (P&D)" as a large-scale SEAT format

Based on the literature review of theories of speaking (chapter 2) and those relevant to SET (chapter 3) and a comparative study of several influential SET formats (chapter 4), and drawing on the findings and experiences of the empirical research project on several SEAT formats (chapter 5), this chapter copes with construction and administration of a "presentation and discussion (P&D)" format for a large-scale SEAT held in Zhejiang University for the second-year non-English majors. This format is constructed according to a candidate-centered cross-cultural thematic approach to SEAT design put forward.

6.1 A candidate-centered cross-cultural thematic approach to SEAT design

Based on the research projects in the previous chapters, a theoretical approach to SEAT design is put forward here, i.e., a candidate-centered cross-cultural thematic approach. Several features of this approach can be stated as follows:

- **Candidate-centeredness:** The SEAT should be designed according to the needs of the candidates, in which the social needs and the syllabus requirements are a part, and should facilitate maximum utterance from the candidates for assessment with minimum interference from the examiners within the practical limitations. This feature favors the interaction among candidates rather than that between the candidate and the examiner. On the contrary, the presence of the examiner should be as invisible as it is possible.

- **Cross-cultural topics:** The SEAT should be able to test the cross-cultural competence as well as the communicative competence. This is preferably achieved through careful selection of cross-cultural topics and test tasks. Moreover, the assessment criteria should also include the cross-cultural dimension.

- **Thematic coherence:** The test tasks should be centered on one broad theme and should encourage in-depth thoughts on the theme.

- **Comprehensible linguistic input:** The candidates should be supplied with sufficient authentic linguistic input specially tailored to be comprehensible to them. In the case of several candidates being tested at the same time, different materials should be available to them to generate information gaps among them. Usually, candidates should be granted sufficient time for them to comprehend the materials and prepare for the speaking. Non-verbal prompt can also be used as a complement for the linguistic input.

- **Usefulness principle:** While the reliability and validity are considered important in traditional tests, the qualities of authenticity, interactiveness, impact and practicality are also significant issues for SEAT design.

6.2 Construction of a presentation and discussion (P&D) format

Based on the candidate-centered cross-cultural thematic approach, a presentation and discussion (P&D) SEAT format is constructed and administered among eight classes of sophomores in Zhejiang University in December 2000 shortly before their final English examination.

Test content

The test includes two major tasks for each candidate. One is presentation and the other is discussion.

Preparation: (10 minutes)

Before the candidates perform the two tasks, each of them is given a test paper, each test paper including a different passage within one broad theme. The passage is between 350 to 400 words long. Each of the candidates is also given a sheet of paper for him to take notes. The candidates are given 10 minutes to read the passage and prepare for the first task. They can use dictionaries, take notes and draft outlines for the presentation, but they are not allowed to communicate with each other, nor are they allowed to write on the test papers since later candidates will use these test papers. At the end of the test, both the test papers and the note sheets are collected.

Test tasks: (10 minutes)

Task 1 Presentation (6 minutes)

The presentation is given within 1.5 minutes and should include at least three parts (This is very similar to the mini-speech format).

1) **Introduction:** This may include greetings, self-introduction,

introduction of the topic to arouse the interest of the audience, presentation of key words and new vocabulary, etc.

2) **Main body:** This part is further divided into two sub-sections. One is called "summary", in which the candidate summarizes the passage guided by the question given. The other is called "relationship", in which the candidate relates what he/she reads to his/her own life.

3) **Conclusion:** Here, the speaker summarizes his speech in a powerful, impressive, or inspirational way.

Part 2 Discussion (4 minutes)

This task is performed by the candidates according to a question given by the examiner.

Topics

Different from the mini-speech discussed in chapter 5, the topic for the P&D SEAT is decided by the test designer. Based on the needs analysis of topics in chapter 5, the P&D SEAT designer chooses two topics for two sets of test papers. Therefore, it also meets the requirements on topics in the mini-speech format (see 5.1.2.2).

Test procedure
Physical setting

One examiner tests four candidates at one sitting. The examiner gives brief instructions, controls the procedure and scores the candidates. They will be seated around a table (ideally a long one) as follows.

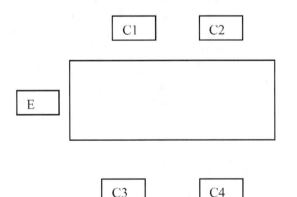

Figure 6.1 The physical setting of the P&D SEAT (C: candidate; E: examiner)

Procedure

The procedure will be done according to the following flow chart.

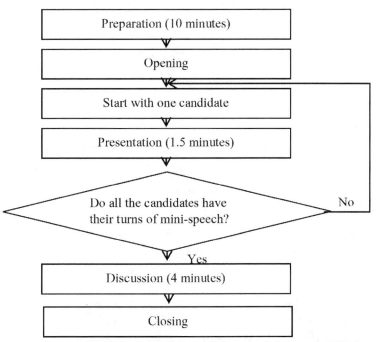

Figure 6.2 The procedural flow chart of mini-speech SET format

Two classrooms are required for this test. When a group begins the test, the next group is in the same classroom. They are given the other set of test papers and are required to prepare for their presentation. At the same time, the rest of the class wait in a nearby classroom watched over by the monitor. This arrangement is planned to avoid leakage of the test content.

Rating method

This test adopts analytical rating method by one assessor. This is for the benefit of higher reliability and for diagnostic purposes. It is very important that the examiners/assessors be trained adequately prior to the test.

Criteria for assessment

The criteria for assessment will be applied not only to the speeches given, but also to the questions and answers between the speaker and the audience.

- Content (Components of the speech complete, main ideas standing out and details substantive)

- Accuracy (Correct use of pronunciation, vocabulary and structure)

- Range (A wide coverage of vocabulary and structure)

- Fluency (Appropriate speed, stress and intonation)

- Discourse management (Cohesion and coherence)

- Register or appropriacy (Use of language appropriate to context, function and intention)

- Strategy (Effective use of linguistic and non-linguistic strategies)

- Cross-cultural competence (Whether the candidates displays sensibility, tolerance to cultural differences and flexibility in dealing with them)

From the above description, it can be seen that this assessment criteria is very similar to those adopted in the mini-speech format (see 5.1.2.2). The only difference is the last criterion. In the mini-speech format, it was "participation". But in P&D, it is "cross-cultural competence". This is not only to stress the importance of cross-cultural competence in oral interaction, but also because the separate criterion of participation is not necessary as it is already included in strategic use.

Rating scale

Similar to the practice in the mini-speech format, the assessment criteria for P&D format are also classified into four groups, and each group is given equal weighting. The difference lies in the descriptions of the new assessment criterion called "cross-cultural competence". Also, to make the marking easier, the assessors are made to give each analytical score according to a 100-point marking system they are most familiar with (see table 6.1). The speaking skill is divided according to traditions in Chinese colleges into five levels which are termed as excellent, good, average, acceptable or pass, poor or failure.

Table 6.1 Rating scale for the P&D SEAT

Scores Degree of skill	Content	Language		Meta-language
	Content	Accuracy and range	Fluency and discourse management	Register, strategy, participation and cross-cultural competence
90-100 Excellent	➢ Components of the speech complete ➢ Main ideas standing out ➢ Details substantive	➢ Correct pronunciation ➢ Correct use of vocabulary and structure ➢ A wide range of vocabulary and structure	➢ Appropriate speed, stress and intonation ➢ Effective use of cohesive devices ➢ Coherence achieved	➢ Use of language appropriate to context, function and intention ➢ Effective use of linguistic and non-linguistic strategies ➢ Very sensitive, tolerant and flexible in dealing with cross-cultural differences
80-89 Good	➢ Lack of necessary components in the subsections of the speech ➢ Main ideas clear but not very powerful ➢ Details stated but not enough	➢ Containing a few pronunciation errors ➢ Containing a few errors in vocabulary and structure ➢ A basically satisfactory range of vocabulary and structure to deal with the topic	➢ A little hasty or slow, some wrong stress and intonation ➢ Adequate use of cohesive devices ➢ Satisfactory logic and coherence	➢ Occasionally containing language too formal or too casual ➢ Satisfactory use of linguistic and non-linguistic strategies ➢ Sensitive, tolerant and flexible in dealing with cross-cultural differences
70-79 Average	➢ Lacking necessary components in the presentation ➢ Main ideas stated but not very powerful ➢ Details stated	➢ Containing pronunciation errors not affecting communication ➢ Containing grammatical errors not affecting communication ➢ Adequate range of vocabulary to convey ideas	➢ Prolonged silence or some wrong stress and intonation ➢ Containing use of cohesive devices ➢ Acceptable logic and coherence	➢ Containing some language too formal or too casual. ➢ Some linguistic and non-linguistic strategies used ➢ Sensitive and tolerant to cultural differences, but not very flexible in dealing with them.
60-69 Acceptable/ pass	➢ Lacking a major subsection in the presentation ➢ Main ideas not clear ➢ Some details irrelevant	➢ Errors of pronunciation affecting communication ➢ Errors of vocabulary and communication affecting communication ➢ A minimum range of vocabulary and structure	➢ Inappropriate speed, wrong stress or intonation affecting communication ➢ Occasional or wrong use of cohesive devices ➢ Cohesion not well achieved	➢ Register of language affecting communication ➢ Occasional or some wrong use of strategies ➢ Sensitive to cultural differences, but not very tolerant to them.
Below 60 Poor or failure	➢ Subsections not obvious ➢ Main ideas not stated ➢ Most details irrelevant or no supporting details	➢ Full of errors on pronunciation ➢ Full of errors on vocabulary and structure ➢ Vocabulary and structure scarce or repetitive	➢ Inability to control speed, full of stress and intonation errors ➢ No use of cohesive devices ➢ Very bad coherence	➢ Register of language cause inability of communication ➢ No or totally wrong use of strategies ➢ Not sensitive to cultural differences at all.

Training of assessors

Before the test, the examiners are trained, which last about two hours. The training procedure is shown as follows.

1) The test designer distributes the test specifications (see appendix 7), the sample test papers (see appendix 9), the examiners' material regulating what the examiner is supposed to say (see appendix 10) and the marking sheet for the examiner. He then explains these materials to them in details.

2) The test designer and examiners talk about the testing syllabuses, especially about the procedure of the tests and the rating scales.

3) A trial test is performed, in which all the examiners score the performance of four sample candidates. The four students are carefully selected by the classroom teacher to represent the whole range of oral levels of the class. The whole trial test is recorded by either a video camera or a tape recorder.

4) The examiners compare, talk about and adjust their scores to reach an agreement. If one candidate is given scores so diverse that they belong to different degrees of skill, his recorded performance is reassessed against the assessment criteria.

5) The test designer summarizes and comments on the training, and then stresses some guidelines to be observed. These guidelines include:

   ● The assessors should refer to the assessment criteria frequently in the beginning period of the test in order to grasp and use the criteria well.

   ● The assessors should adhere to the rating standard through the whole testing process. To be specific, they should avoid the central tendency during the mid- and end- period of testing. The central tendency refers to the trend of giving lower scores to candidates of excellent degree and giving higher scores to those of poor degree. This tendency often occurs in the mid- and end-period of subjective testing such as a writing test (杨惠中 & Weir, 1998: 149).

   ● The examiner/assessor should be able to control the time of each test task. Former practice reveals that candidates tend to use more time than they are given. Although the longer the utterance, the better candidates' competence is displayed. However, due to the limitations of practicality, their utterance should be kept within the time limit. Occasionally, however, candidates could be allowed to exceed the time limit a little bit if they seem to finish their turn very soon or if the assessor feels not confident enough in deciding their marks. But the assessor should remember that s long as candidates display enough utterance for assessment, he should try to stop them in case they might make long speeches and keep the others waiting.

6.3 Administration of the P&D SEAT

The administration of the P&D SEAT involves the following procedures.

1) Preparing test papers

Two sets of test papers are prepared so that when one group of candidates is tested, the next group can read the materials and prepare for their presentation. For each set of test papers, a test syllabus for the examiner is also prepared to regulate what the examiner is supposed to say during the test.

2) Writing test syllabuses for examiners and candidates

The test syllabuses are written for training of examiners and candidates

3) Designing the questionnaire for candidates

The questionnaire is supposed to investigate into candidates' views on SET and their comments on P&D format.

4) Informing and training candidates

The candidates are informed of the testing syllabus two weeks in advance. Relevant questions of the candidates are answered. In the present study, candidates are also told that their SET scores would be filed and will account for ten percent of their final English scores of the term. Afterwards, they are given a brief training. This is carried out easily because presentation and discussion are two activities students participate in frequently in the classroom.

5) Training examiners/assessors

6) Carrying out the test

7) Questionnaire survey

After the test, the candidates answer the questionnaire at once.

8)   Analysis of test results

The analysis of the test results is illustrated in the next chapter.

9)   Reporting the test results

Chapter 7 Phase two study: evaluation of the usefulness of the P&D SEAT format

7.1 Introduction

Test evaluation is necessary for decision making based upon the test results and for further research and improvement of the test. This chapter tries to evaluate the usefulness of the P&D SEAT format against the criteria of usefulness given by Bachman and Palmer (1996: 17-42). Particularly, the qualities of validity, reliability and practicality are analyzed in detail because these qualities are considered the most important and are hard to achieve by the researcher.

7.2 Methodology

Subjects

The subjects are 48 band-4 students in Zhejiang University (Yuquan Campus). To evaluate the reliability of the P&D SEAT format, candidates' scores of end-term examination in the form of a written test is collected. This examination is held a week after the spoken English test. A CET-SET is also conducted immediately after the P&D SEAT in order to evaluate the concurrent validity of the P&D SEAT format. After both tests, a questionnaire survey is conducted on the candidates to reveal the candidates' opinions on the test.

Methods

Statistical analysis of test results and of the questionnaire survey is carried out to evaluate the P&D SEAT formats. To be specific, correlations between P&D SEAT results and end-term examinations are calculated to evaluate the reliability of the P&D format. This method is based on a accepted assumption that subjective tests of candidates' competence should bear a considerable correlation with the objective test (桂诗春, 1986: 168; 杨惠中 & Weir, 1998: 41). Correlations between P&D SEAT results and CET-SET results are calculated to judge the concurrent validity of the P&D formats. Afterwards, the teacher time per student (TT/S) is calculated to show how practical the P&D format. Finally, the statistical analysis of the questionnaire survey is conducted to reveal candidates' opinions on the

P&D format.

7.3 Results and discussion

7.3.1 Test results

Reliability

To evaluate the reliability of the P&D format, the correlations among P&D, CET-SET and the end-term examination are shown in table 7.1.

Table 7.1 The correlations among P&D, CET-SET and the end-term examination

	P&D	CET-SET	Objective	Writing	Final	Reported final
P&D	1					
CET-SET	0.535	1				
Objective	0.460	0.164	1			
Writing	0.662	0.436	0.529	1		
Final	0.551	0.245	0.979	0.692	1	
Reported final	0.651	0.266	0.927	0.742	0.968	1

Table 7.1 shows that P&D format is a reliable test because the test results bear acceptable correlations with the end-term examination results. If a subjective test, such as writing, bears a correlation of higher than 0.4 with the objective test, then it is considered reliable (杨惠中 & Weir, 1998: 41). The correlation between the P&D SEAT results and the objective test in the end-term examination is 0.460, which is higher than 0.4, therefore, the P&D SEAT format is a reliable test. The reliability of the P&D format is further testified by its correlations with the writing part, the total end-term examination and the reported scores[9].

---

[9] The end-term examination is composed of objective test items (listening, reading, vocabulary and structure and close) and a writing test, the latter occupying 15% of the total score. In the reported score for the term, the end-term score occupies 70%, the other 30% are evenly distributed to the P&D SEAT score, the mid-term examination score and the teacher's judgement of classroom performance.

It can be seen that P&D scores have very high correlation with the writing. This indicates that speaking and writing, both being considered as productive skills, are closely related.

Ironically, the CET-SET, which is considered as an established SET format, has a low correlation (0.164) with the objective test. This might suggest that it might be less reliable than the P&D format. This is probably attributed to the different rating method adopted by the CET-SET. As is well known, it adopts a 15-point rating scale, and each sub-criterion in the rating scale occupies 5 points. This is a little bit rough for the differentiation of candidates' oral competence. Although it is generally considered difficult to distinguish candidates' oral competence, the assessors report that it is still possible to see the differences between candidates. The P&D adopts a 100-point rating scale and this enables more elaborate differentiation among candidates.

Another reason for the unsatisfactory reliability of CET-SET might be concerned with the band description of CET-SET, which is illustrated in table 7.2.

Table 7.2 Band descriptions of CET-SET

Bands	Band descriptions
A+(14.5-15) A(13.5-14.4)	Having no difficulty in oral communication on familiar topics
B+(12.5-13.4) B(11-12.4)	Having difficulty in oral communication on familiar topics, but the communication is successful.
C+(9.5-10.9) C(8-9.4)	Capable of simple oral communication on familiar topics
D(below 7.9)	Having no oral competence

This band description is different from the traditional practice in Chinese colleges. The convention of rating in Chinese colleges is to give 100-point marks and candidates' marks are classified into five bands (see table 7.3)

Table 7.3 The convention of the course rating system in Chinese colleges

Bands	Excellent	Good	Average	Acceptable or pass	Failure
Scores	90-100	80-89.5	70-79.5	60-69.5	Below 60

The P&D format adopts the traditional rating method and band description to reveal the requirements of achievement tests. Probably this is why its scores are more comparable and therefore has higher correlations with the end-term examination.

However, the above reasons remain as hypotheses to be justified by later research projects.

One defect with this research is that it is not possible to evaluate the inter-rater reliability. This is because the test is conducted within each class for the sake of administrative practicality; hence the candidates are not randomly sampled and distributed to assessors. However, this defect remains to be overcome in future research.

Validity

The evaluation of the validity of the P&D SEAT format is based upon two basic assumptions. One is that speaking should be more related to writing, which is also a productive skill. The other is that P&D SEAT format should be highly related to CET-SET, which is an established format of SET. Therefore, the correlations between P&D and test results of other skills are also calculated (see table 7.4).

Table 7.4 Correlations between P&D and test results of other skills

	Listening	Reading	Vocabulary	Cloze	Writing	Final	P&D	CET-SET
Listening	1							
Reading	0.229	1						
Vocabulary	0.012	0.381	1					
Cloze	-0.006	0.424	0.381	1				
Writing	-0.018	0.489	0.386	0.548	1			
Final	0.371	0.893	0.597	0.626	0.692	1		
P&D	**-0.054**	**0.422**	**0.549**	**0.258**	**0.662**	**0.550**	1	
CET-SET	-0.106	0.254	0.068	0.047	0.436	0.245	**0.536**	1

Table 7.4 shows that the P&D SEAT results have a very high correlation with writing (0.662). Meanwhile, the correlation between P&D and CET-SET is also very high (0.536). In this sense, P&D format is considered valid.

From table 7.4, several other interesting findings are also revealed. It seems that P&D format also has high correlations with vocabulary and structure (0.546) and reading (0.422). The high correlation with vocabulary and structure may indicate that P&D format is able to explore the vocabulary range because it involves deep thinking over a thought-provoking topic. The high correlation with reading could be due

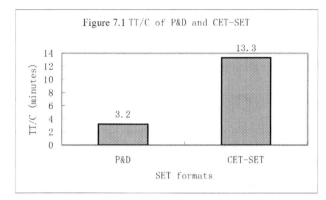

to the fact that this format requires reading of a passage in the preparation stage of the presentation. These features of P&D format might have positive impact on teaching in that one of the major purposes of our English teaching is to enlarge the vocabulary by encouraging reading and thought-provoking activities.

To further survey the validity of the P&D format, its correlations with the ranking of oral ability in the class by both the teacher and the candidates themselves are calculated (see table 7.5)

Table 7.5 Correlations between the P&D SEAT and rankings by the teacher and the candidates.

	T's ranking	Cs' ranking	P&D ranking
T's ranking	1		
Cs' ranking	0.654	1	
P&D ranking	0.767	0.427	1

From table 7.5, we can see that the P&D format has very high correlation (0.767) with the teacher's ranking of candidates' oral competence. However, its correlation with candidates' ranking is a little lower than that with the teacher's ranking. This is probably because of the inaccuracy of judgments of the candidates because of their different personalities. Some candidates might be very optimistic and tend to over-estimate their oral competence while others may be more modest and tend to under-estimate their oral competence. However, this still remains as a hypothesis to be further testified.

Practicality and efficiency

Practicality

The practicality of the test is calculated in terms of the teacher time per student (TT/S) since the most scant resources are lack of teacher time in such an achievement test. The TT/S of P&D format is calculated together with that of CET-SET for the sake of comparison (see figure 7.1).

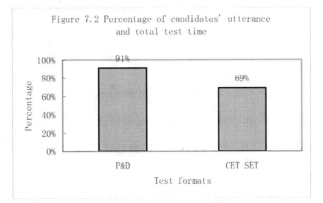

Figure 7.2 Percentage of candidates' utterance and total test time

From figure 7.1 we can see that the P&D format is far more practical than CET-SET. Interview with assessors also reveal that the TT/S of P&D can be further reduced to around 2.5 minutes if this format is more familiar with the examiners and the candidates. This means that the P&D SEAT could be conducted within two class hours for a class of around 40 students. This means that the P&D format satisfies the requirement of practicality very well.

Efficiency

To further evaluate the efficiency of this test format, the length of the candidates' utterance is also calculated (see table 7.6). This is based on another assumption that a good SET should facilitate as much candidates' utterance as possible within the test time.

Figure 7.2 shows that 91% of the test time is occupied with candidates' utterance in P&D format. This is because the P&D format is candidate-centered while the examiner is required to be as invisible as possible except for ensuring the procedure of the test. In CET-SET, however, only 69% of the test time is devoted to candidates' performance. This means that 31% of the test time is dominated by the examiner, who keeps asking questions and giving directions. In this sense, the P&D format is not much more efficient.

7.3.2 Questionnaire

The questionnaire is designed to include two parts. Part one is intended to investigate the general beliefs of candidates on SET. Part two attempts to survey candidates' evaluation of both the P&D format and CET-SET.

Part one: General beliefs of candidates on SET

The first question in this part is for the purpose of validity evaluation of P&D against candidates' own ranking of their oral competence and is already talked about in the above discussion on validity. Therefore this question is left out here. Four other questions to be discussed here are as follows:

- Do you think it necessary to have an SEAT in the end of a term?
- Which test type do you prefer, the direct or indirect test?
- Do you prefer to talk with other candidates or to talk with the examiner during a direct test?
- Do you wish to be provided with reading materials related to the topic prior to the test?

Responses to these questions will be analyzed respectively here.

Direct or indirect SET?

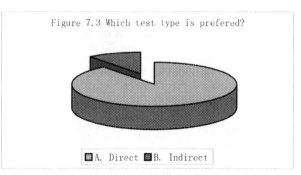

Figure 7.3 Which test type is prefered?

A. Direct ■ B. Indirect

Figure 7.3 shows that the majority of candidates prefer the direct SEAT.

Table 7.6 Reasons for the direct test type

Reason for direct test type	Number	Percentage
1) Unwilling to talk to the machine because machines do not have feelings.	19	50%
2) It is less nervous talking to people than speaking with a machine.	8	21%
3) A direct test is more authentic.	29	76%
4) A direct test enables multi-turn bi-directional interaction, while an indirect test does not.	20	53%
5) Other reasons	3	8%

Table 7.6 shows that candidates prefer a direct test because it is more authentic, enables multi-turn bi-directional interaction and sharing of feelings.

Peer group communication or candidate-examiner communication?

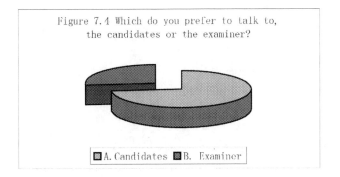

Figure 7.4 Which do you prefer to talk to, the candidates or the examiner?

☐ A. Candidates ■ B. Examiner

Figure 7.4 suggests that the majority of candidates prefer to talk to other candidates rather than the examiner.

Table 7.7 Reasons why candidates prefer to talk within peer groups

Reason for why candidates prefer to talk within peer groups	Number	Percentage
1) It is less nervous talking with candidates rather than with the examiner.	15	39%
2) Candidates are similar in age and experiences; therefore they have a lot in common to talk about.	22	58%
3) Candidates can encourage each other.	17	45%

Table 7.7 shows that candidates like to talk among themselves mainly because they are similar in age and experiences and have a lot in common.

Necessity of linguistic input

Table 7.8 shows that most candidates believe adequate linguistic input enables them to prepare on both content (what to say) and language (how to say it) in case they might have nothing to say on the topic. This is of significance for a SET, because if candidates have nothing to say, how could their oral competence be measured?

Table 7.8 Reasons for necessity of linguistic input

Reasons for necessity of linguistic input	Number	Percentage
1) Adequate linguistic input enables candidates to prepare on both content and language in case that they might have nothing to say on the topic.	21	55%
2) Other reasons	2	5%

However, some people might argue that if the topics are carefully chosen to be within the candidates' knowledge structure, they are able to say something without the linguistic input. In this aspect, I would argue that even such topics are chosen they tend to bias in favor of some candidates and against others. For example, in the CET-SET sample test

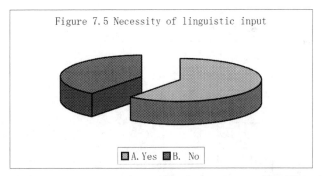

Figure 7.5 Necessity of linguistic input

A. Yes B. No

paper, candidates are required to talk about city traffic. This is carefully chosen because most of the universities are located in cities. Therefore students are familiar with the topic. However, if a poor student from the countryside (which not a rare case in Chinese universities) is asked on the differences between private cars and taxis, he might have nothing to say because he had never taken a taxi nor owned a private car, nor did he ever think about them, simply because these are two expensive and not within his consideration at all. In this case, some linguistic input is necessary. In other cases, the linguistic input is also indispensable when candidates

115

knows what to say, but they simply are not able to express them well because they lack the vocabulary of one or two important items.

But is this practice "authentic" enough? It is well known that prior to any presentation, the speaker has to do some reading (in other words, literature research) before the presentation. This does not include the various kinds of reading he has done already long before the presentation is held. In this sense, the practice of providing linguistic input is authentic.

Part two: candidates' evaluation of both the P&D format and CET-SET

In this part, four issues are surveyed. They are the use of strategies, the quality of performance, the appropriacy of the linguistic input and the overall evaluation on the two SET formats.

Use of strategies

The investigation on strategies is conducted for two purposes. One is to find out whether candidates employ certain strategies in the test. In this sense, we can also see whether the two SET facilitate strategic competence. The other purpose is to identify whether the strategies candidates use are contributory or not. Based on studies on strategies on language learning and use, 13 strategies are surveyed, among which seven are contributory and six are noncontributory (see 2.2 for theoretical discussion on strategies).

Table 7.9 Statistical analysis of strategic use in both P&D and CET-CET

Strategy		P&D						CET-SET					
		1	2	3	4	5	Mean	1	2	3	4	5	Mean
Contributory	B	2	4	6	17	8	3.68	26	0	4	4	3	1.86
	C	1	5	10	15	6	3.54	5	4	8	12	8	3.38
	E	2	5	6	18	5	3.53	2	2	8	16	8	3.72
	G	4	7	15	8	2	2.92	4	9	12	10	1	2.86
	H	5	7	11	12	2	2.97	6	7	12	10	2	2.86
	L	1	0	2	19	15	4.27	2	1	4	18	12	4.00
	M	12	6	5	7	7	2.76	11	6	5	8	7	2.84
Noncontribut	A	6	9	6	11	4	2.94	26	5	2	2	1	1.53
	D	10	20	1	3	2	2.08	10	15	3	6	2	2.31

		1	2	3	4	5	Mean	1	2	3	4	5	Mean
F		7	14	7	8	0	2.44	12	12	7	6	0	2.19
I		7	19	3	5	3	2.41	7	18	4	6	2	2.41
J		9	12	10	4	1	2.33	9	13	8	5	1	2.33
K		7	18	7	5	0	2.27	8	18	6	5	0	2.22

Table 7.9 shows that candidates did use some of these strategies. It also reveals that Both SET formats encourage contributory strategic use in general because all the means of noncontributory strategies are below 3, which indicates that candidates basically did not use these strategies. However, we can see that P&D format encourages four contributory strategies (B, C, E, and L), CET-SET encourages only three (C, E, and L). The two SET formats differ in the use of strategy B, which is the use of note-taking and outline-drafting prior to the presentation. This difference suggests that P&D format more favorable than CET-SET in this sense because note-taking and outline-drafting are useful skills both in the learning of English and later use of English.

Quality of performance

Table 7.10 Candidates' self-judgment on the quality of their performance.

P&D						CET-SET					
1	2	3	4	5	Mean	1	2	3	4	5	Mean
2	6	22	6	1	2.95	3	7	19	6	2	2.92

Table 7.10 shows that in both formats, candidates reported that they had displayed their average oral competence because the means of their responses is roughly equal to 3.

Appropriacy of linguistic input

Table 7.11 Candidates responses on the linguistic input in the P&D SEAT format

Questions	Choice	Number	Percentage
Is the topic interesting to you?	Yes	21	55%
	No	17	45%
Are you familiar with the vocabulary?	Yes	35	92%
	No	3	8%

How is the difficulty?	Appropriate	32	84%
	Too difficult	4	11%
	Too easy	2	5%
How is the length?	Just right	24	63%
	Too long	3	8%
	Too short	11	29%

Table 7.11 shows that candidates believe that the linguistic input is appropriate in terms of vocabulary range, difficulty and length. More than half of the candidates consider the topic interesting. However, 45 percent of them still see the topic as not interesting enough. Although the topics chosen were based on needs analysis, they still turn out to be difficult to satisfy everyone. But in the future practice, this aspect could be improved by more careful needs analysis and more thorough literature review.

Overall evaluation

Table 7.12 Candidates overall evaluation of the two SET formats

P&D						CET-SET					
1	2	3	4	5	Mean	1	2	3	4	5	Mean
0	1	14	10	5	3.63	0	2	11	11	6	3.70

Table 7.12 shows that candidates are very satisfied at both SET formats.

In this subsection, candidates are also required to remark on the advantages and disadvantages of the two SET formats and to advise on possible improvements. Although their opinions are too diversified to be analyzed and classified, the researcher is able to identify one widespread idea, that is, 12 candidates (32%) believe that the most obvious advantage of the P&D format is that it enables adequate preparation so that candidates are confident in what they want to say.

7.4 A summary of this chapter

This chapter adopts statistical analysis of test results and a questionnaire survey to evaluate the P&D SEAT format. The following conclusions could be drawn.
1) P&D is a highly practical and efficient format for an SEAT and achieves favorable reliability and validity. In this sense, it is a "useful"

test.

2) P&D is in accordance with candidates' beliefs on SET. To be specific, candidates believe it is necessary to have an SEAT at the end of each term. Moreover, candidates favor direct an SEAT which features the interaction among candidates and provision of linguistic input. The P&D format satisfies these requirements.

3) Candidates generally appreciate the P&D format in that they use more contributory strategies than noncontributory ones, display their average oral competence and consider the linguistic input appropriate.

4) Two issues need further efforts for the later use of P&D format. One is that if P&D is used as a large-scale SEAT, it is necessary to consider whether it is possible to calculate the inter-rater reliability. The other is that the topics for later tests should be carefully chosen to be more interesting to the candidates.

Chapter 8 Conclusion

8.1 Major contributions of the present study

In the introduction of this book, it is claimed that the present study attempts to solve the problem of "practicality" of an SEAT to cater to "practical" needs from both society and the non-English majors for an SEAT. So far, I feel confident to announce that this book has, to a considerable degree, solved this problem by means of a literature review and an empirical study. Here below are the major contributions this book has made:

1) A new model of cross-cultural communicative competence for language testing is established, in which both communicative competence (linguistic, pragmatic and strategic) and cross-cultural competence (sensibility, tolerance and flexibility) are encompassed. Strategic competence includes both language learning and use strategies. Moreover, this model illustrates the relationship between competence and knowledge.

2) A literature review of theories and practice indicates that a direct, criteria-referenced test type is preferable to an indirect, norm-referenced one for the construction of an SEAT, that linguistic input of cross-cultural topics is favorably supplied to candidates, and that the analytical rating method is better than the holistic method in terms of reliability and for the analytical purpose.

3) A contrastive study of four SEAT formats confirms the findings of the literature review. Moreover, empirical evidence also suggests that the inter-rater reliability is high enough to allow the one-assessor model to be adopted in an SEAT, that content is a necessary assessment criterion, that mini-speech, which mainly resembles the oral presentation technique, is more favorable than the role-play and the machine-mediated test for an SEAT.

4) A cross-cultural candidate-centered thematic approach to an SEAT is presented by summarizing previous research. This approach favors the cross-cultural topics and situations, encourages interaction among candidates and requires test tasks in one test to be centered on one broad theme.

5) Finally, an SEAT format, namely, the presentation and discussion (P&D), is constructed according to the cross-cultural candidate-centered thematic approach. It is administered in a class of sophomores in Zhejiang University. Empirical analysis shows that this format meets the requirements of validity, reliability and practicality, thus is a "useful" test.

8.2 Implications for further research

The present study is far from a once-and-for-all resolution to the SEAT. Further research should be conducted to deal with the following remaining problems.

1) The model of cross-cultural communicative competence is not able to reveal the relationship between "competence" and "proficiency". As is well known, having competence does not necessarily mean being able to perform well. But what are the differences between the two terms of "competence" and "proficiency"? What factors may affect the performance of a candidate?

2) The discussion on "strategic competence" in the present study is far from adequate. It classifies strategies candidates employ in SET into contributory and noncontributory ones. The former is further divided into language learning strategies and language use strategies. But what language learning strategies are also contributory to language use and what are not? What language use strategies are also contributory to language learning and what are not? What's more, in the investigation of strategies employed in our test, the division between contributory and noncontributory is based on previous studies on "good" language learners. But what strategies do "poor" language learners employ? What strategies do "harm" rather than "good" to language learning or use? Under what circumstances?

3) Reliability is evaluated by calculation of correlations between the SEAT and the written tests and the teacher's subjective assessment of candidates. But this is not enough. In the present study, neither inter-rater reliability nor intra-rater reliability is tackled quantitatively.

4) A problem closely related to the last question is one of score modification. The present study does not attempt to modify the scores given by the assessors because the inter-rater reliability and intra-rater

reliability is not quantitatively analyzed. Of course, strict examiner training procedure is emphasized and administered to reduce the assessment errors. But what has to be done if there is a large difference in adhering to the assessment criteria between two assessors or in one assessor in the process of testing? Do the SEAT scores need to be modified? If the answer to the last question is positive, then how?

These questions are not discussed in the present study due to the limitations of time and the researcher's abilities. However, if a large-scale SEAT is to be conducted widely, it is impossible to avoid these questions.

References

Bachman, L. F. & Palmer, Aldrian. S. (1996). *Language Testing in Practice*. Oxford: Oxford University Press.

Bachman, L. F. (1990). *Fundamental Considerations in Language Testing*. Oxford: Oxford University Press.

Brown, H.D. (1980), *Principles of Language Learning and Testing*, Englewood Cliffs, N.J.: Prentice-Hall, Inc.

Bygate, M. (1987). *Speaking*. Oxford: Oxford University Press

Canale, M. & Swain, M. (1980). Theoretical bases of communicative approaches to second language teaching and testing. *Applied Linguistics*. 1, 1-47.

Canale, M. (1983). On some dimensions of language proficiency. In J. Oller (Eds.), *Issues in Language Testing Research*. Rowley. MA: Newbury House.

CHEN, Y. (2000). A multiple-method classroom approach to testing oral proficiency. Unpublished term paper for the course of Language Testing as part of requirements for MA degree in Linguistics and Applied Linguistics in Zhejiang University.

Cohen, A. D. (1998). *Strategies in Learning and Using a Second Language*. Addison Wesley Longman Limited.

Dale, P & Wolf, J. C. (1988). *Speech Communication for International Students*. Englewood Cliffs: Prentice Hall Regents.

Davies, S. & R. West. (1989). *The Longman Guide to English Language Examinations*. Essex: Longman Group UK Limited.

Educational Testing Service. (1998). *TOEFL 1998-1999 Information Bulletin for TOEFL, TWE and TSE*. New Jersey: ETS.

Heaton, J. B. (1988). *Writing English Language Tests*. New York: Longman Group UK Limited.

Hong Kong Examinations Authority. (1996). *HKDLE question papers*. Hong Kong: Hong Kong Examinations Authority.

Howe, D. H. (1983). *New Access*. Hong Kong: Oxford University Press.

Hubbard, P. et al. (1983). *A Training Course for TEFL*. Oxford: Oxford University Press.

Hymes, D. H. (1972). On communicative competence. In J. B. Pride & J. Holmes (Eds.), *Sociolinguistics* , 269-293. Harmondsworth: Penguin.

Krashen, S. (1985). *The Input Hypothesis: Issues and Implications*. London: Longman.

Lado, R. (1961). *Language Testing*. New York: McGraw Hill.

Nunan, D. (1993). *Designing Tasks for the Communicative Classroom*. Cambridge: CUP.

O'Malley, J.M. & Chamot, A. U. (1990). *Learning Strategies in Second Language Acquisition*. Cambridge: Cambridge University Press.

Oxford, R. (1990). *Language Learning Strategies: What Every Teacher Should Know*. New York: Newbury House Publishers.

Rubin, J. (1975). What the 'good' language learner can teach us. *TESOL Quarterly*. (9), 41-51.

Spolsky, B. (1995). *Measured Words*. Oxford: Oxford University Press.

Swain, M. (1984). Large-scale communicative language testing: a case study. In S. J. Savingnon & M. S. Berns (Eds.). *Initiatives in Communicative Language Teaching*. Reading MA: Addison Wesley.

Swain, M. (1995). Three functions of output in second language learning. In Cook, G & B. Seidlhofer (Eds.). *Principles and Practice in Applied Linguistics*. Oxford: Oxford University Press.

Underhill, N. (1987). *Testing Spoken Language: a Handbook of Oral Testing Techniques*. Cambridge: Cambridge University Press.

Walker, C. (1990). Large-scale oral testing. *Applied Linguistics, 11* (2), 200-219.

Weir, C. J. (1990). *Communicative Language Testing*. Prentice Hall International (UK) Ltd.

Weir, C. J. (1993). *Understanding and Developing Language Tests*. Prentice Hall.

White,V. R. (1985). *The English Teacher's Handbook*. Thomas Nelson & Sons Ltd.

XU, Li-sheng. (1998). *Aspects of Intercultural Communication: a New Reader*. Unpublished textbook for MA candidates of Linguistics, College of Foreign Languages, Zhejiang University.

桂诗春. (1986). *标准化考试——理论、原则与方法*. 广州: 广东高等教育出版社.

韩宝成. (2000). 语言测试: 理论、实践与发展. *外语教学与研究*. (1).

贾志高. (1998). 从剑桥英语交际技能考试看交际英语测试的特点. *外语界*. (3).

教育部高等教育司. (2007). *大学英语课程教学要求*. 北京: 高等教育出版社.

李筱菊. (1997). *语言测试科学与艺术*. 长沙: 湖南教育出版社.

廉洁. (1998). 制约学习策略的学习者因素. *外语与外语教学*. (6).

刘润清. (1991). *语言测试和它的方法*. 北京: 外语教学与研究出版社.

罗伟. (1999). 大学英语教学模式的本质与模式验证–兼评应惠兰等的主题教学模式. *外语教学与研究*. (4）.

秦晓晴. (1998). 硕士研究生使用英语学习策略特点的实证研究. *外语教学*. (1).

全国大学英语四、六级考试委员会. (1999). *大学英语口语考试大纲及样题*. 上海: 上海外语教育出版社.

舒运祥. (1999). *外语测试的理论和方法*. 上海: 世界图书出版公司.

外语界. (1999). 简讯: 大学英语口语考试试点取得成功. 即将全面推开. *外语界*. (3).

文秋芳. (1996). *英语学习策略论*. 上海: 上海外语教育出版社.

文秋芳. (1999). *英语口语测试与教学*. 上海: 上海外语教育出版社.

吴一安, 刘润清. (1993). 中国英语本科学生素质调查报告. *外语教学与研究*. (1).

徐海铭.2006. 口语测试的理论、设计、实施和研究-《二语口语测试》评述. *外语与外语教学*. (1).

许力生. (1998). *新编跨文化交际学选读（Aspects of Intercultural Communication）*. 98 级英语语言学和应用语言学硕士研究生教材. 未正式出版.

杨惠中, Weir, C. (1998). *大学英语四、六级考试效度研究*. 上海: 上海外语教育出版社.

杨惠中. (1999). 大学英语口语考试设计原则. *外语界*. (3).

杨惠中. (1999). 语言测试与语言教学. *外语界*. (1).

杨莉芳. (2006). 近二十年口语测试研究中存在的主要问题. *外语教学. 27* (1).

应惠兰, 何莲珍, 周颂波. (1998). 大学公共英语教学改革-以学生为中心的主题教学模式. *外语教学与研究*. (4).

张文忠, 郭晶晶. (2002). 模糊评分: 外语口语测试评分新思路. *现代外语,* (1).

Appendix 1 A complete test paper for HKEA-SET (HKEA, 1996: 57).

Part one Individual presentation (1.5-2 minutes each; total time: 8 minutes)

Read the following passage. You may take notes to use as the basis for your presentation. If you wish, you can add you own opinions or ideas.

Kidnapped teachers in the Philippines

Religious extremists in the Philippines have recently kidnapped at least 28 teachers in a series of incidents which took place about 800 kilometers south of Manila. All the teachers were wither rescued by the army or were released when their families paid money to the kidnappers. However, teachers remain in fear of similar incidents and they are worried that before long a kidnapped teacher may be killed.

Educational officials in the Philippines have stated that they may have to close all schools because of the risk of further kidnappings. Classes at three schools have already been suspended because about 200 teachers are refusing to go to work. The teachers have complained that the local government and the army are not doing enough to maintain law and order in the region. They are not willing to work unless the government can guarantee their safety.

It is not clear why the group of religious extremists is choosing teachers as a target for its terrorist activities. Some experts believe that the lack of security in the schools makes the teachers particularly vulnerable. Others point out that the kidnapping of teachers is only part of a wider campaign of violence, which includes bombings and murders across the whole of the southern Philippines.

If all schools in the region do have to be closed, it would affect the education of thousands of children. Although education officials what schools to run normally, they understand the teachers' fears. The regional education director pointed out that there was little he could do if teachers refused to work. He is urging the government to send more soldiers to the area to protect the teachers. It is hoped that this will enable schools to return to normal in the near future.

Part two Group discussion (total time: 12 minutes)

The Young Post has invited students to write and edit articles for a special issue of the newspaper. The theme of this issue will be the problems facing schools in Hong Kong and other parts of the world.

You are a member of the editorial committee responsible for producing this issue of the newspaper. You will probably want to discuss which countries and which problems to focus on as well as to make some recommendations about how the problems can be dealt with.

You do not need to come to a final decision or to reach a conclusion to your discussion. You should try to discuss both the content and procedures involved in your discussion task. You cannot take notes or write during the discussion.

The examiners cannot answer any questions about the instructions or the task you have to discuss. If you have any question, you may discuss them among yourselves and that will be an acceptable part of your group discussion which will be assessed.

Appendix 2 A complete test paper of TEM-SET(文秋芳, 1999: 235)

There are usually two set of test papers. The following is the second set for TEM-SET held in 1998.

Task I: Retell a story

The Amazing Discovery

There is a story of the Washington family. The father of the present Mr. Washington had been a direct descendant of George Washington. At the close of the American Civil War, he was a twenty-five-year-old colonel left with about a thousand dollars in gold.

The young colonel decided to go West to try his luck. When he had been in Montana for less than a month and things were going very poorly indeed, he came upon his great discovery.

He had lost his way when riding in the hills, and after a day without food, he began to grow hungry. He saw a small animal nearby–a squirrel. As he was without his gun, he had to chase it. He noticed that the squirrel was holding something shiny in its mouth. Just before it disappeared into its hole, the little animal dropped its burden. It was a large and perfect diamond.

Late that night, he found his way back to camp and brought all his slaves with him to dig for more diamonds. To his complete amazement, the mountain was diamond – it was nothing else but solid diamond. He filled four bags full of glittering samples and rode back to town. There he managed to sell half a dozen small stones. When he tried a larger one, a storekeeper fainted and he was arrested for disturbing the peace. He escaped from prison and caught the train to New York. There he sold a few medium-sized diamonds and received about two hundred thousand dollars in gold. But he did not dare sell more – in fact, he left New York just in time. People began to talk about a diamond mine being discovered, and soon everyone wanted to go in search of diamonds. But by that time, he was on his way back to Montana. (304 words)

Task II: Imagine your neighbor has become an upstart. Please describe how he/she has become rich so quickly.

Task III: Role-play

Student A: You have decided to take a trip to Yellow Mountain with your classmates during summer holidays but your parents are strongly against it. Now you go to your friend to seek her/his advice on how you can make your parents grant your request. She/he is trying to give you various suggestions. Although her /his suggestions appear to be reasonable, you don't think they can work very well with your parents. **Remember you should start the conversation.**

Student B: Your best friend has decided to take a trip to Yellow Mountain with her/his classmates during summer holidays but her/his parents are strongly against it. She/he comes to you for advice. You are trying to give her/him suggestions on how she/he can make her/his parents grant her/his request. Although your suggestions appear to be reasonable, your friend doesn't think they can work very well with her/his parents. **Remember it is your partner who starts the conversation.**

Appendix 3 A sample test paper of CET-SET (全国大学英语四、六级考试委员会，1999)

Part I (5 minutes)

After each candidate gives a brief self-introduction of no more than 30 seconds, they are required to talk something about their life in the city. The questions the chief examiner may ask include:

1) How do you like living in Beijing (Shanghai, Nanjing ...)?
2) What do you think is the most serious challenge of living in a city like Beijing (Shanghai, Nanjing ...)?
3) How do you like shopping in a supermarket?
4) Where would you like to live, downtown or in the suburbs, and why?
5) What measures do you think we should take to reduce air pollution in Beijing (Shanghai, Nanjing ...)?
6) Can you say something about the entertainment available in your city?
7) Where would you like to find a job after graduation, in a big city like Beijing or Shanghai or in a small town and why?
8) What's your impression of the people in Beijing (Shanghai, Nanjing ...)? / How do you like the people in Beijing (Shanghai, Nanjing ...)?

Part II (10 minutes)
Individual presentations (5 minutes)

In this subsection each candidate is provided with a picture showing two different types of transport. They are given 1 minute for preparation and then are required to give a brief description of each type and then compare the two types. (On the first picture, the types of transport are the private car and the taxi, on the second one, the bus and the subway, on the third one, the bicycle and the motorcycle)

Discussion (5 minutes)

Later, the candidates are required to discuss on which is the best type of transport for a city like Beijing (Shanghai, Nanjing ...).

Part III (5 minutes)

Each candidate is asked one more question for examiners to confirm their oral competence. The questions the chief examiner may ask are:

1) During the discussion, why did you say that ...?
2) What kind of transport do you usually use in your city?
3) Do you have any suggestions as to how traffic conditions can be improved in big cities?
4) Do you think private cars should be encouraged?
5) Why do you think some Western countries encourage people to ride

bicycles?

Appendix 4 A sample test paper of YU-SET (Walker, 1990)

Part I: Questions and answers on the set readers covered in the teaching program.

In this part, the interviewer asks 1 or 2 'general' questions then, perhaps, 2 'specific' questions on each of the books prescribed:

Book 1 The Pearl

Book 2 any two of these marked "*"

> The Road to Nowhere*
>
> The Great Gatsby*
>
> The Woman who Disappeared*

Examples of questions on set books
General:

1) What do you think of the character of X?
2) Describe the character of X.
3) What happens after the part in the book when …?
4) What do you think we could learn from the story?
5) Describe the settings of X.
6) How would you compare (X and Y in) the two books A and B?
7) What do you like/dislike about the story?
8) Who wrote X?
9) What about the language? What did you think of that?

Specific

The Pearl

1) Why didn't the doctor want to see Coyotito?
2) Why did the doctor change his mind about seeing Coyotito?
3) Why did the pearl make Kino everybody's enemy?
4) Why didn't Juana like the pearl?
5) Why didn't the buyers offer a good price for the pearl?
6) Why did someone attack Kino?
7) Do you think that selling the pearl would have made Kino happy?
8) What was worse than killing a man in Kino's village?
9) What did Kino see in the pearl when he looked at it for the last time?
10) Why did Kino decide to throw the pearl into the sea?

(Specific questions for other books are omitted here.)

Part II: Conversation on a given topic

In this part, the interviewer chooses a topic from one of three topic lists and uses the topic to guide students through the language functions as follow:

List of topics:

List A: education, holidays, places, work

List B: accommodation, leisure, past events, personal information

List C: Daily life, language study, money and possessions, travel and transport

List of language functions (taken from the syllabus):

➢ Describing

➢ Clarifying

➢ Asking questions (1)

➢ Exemplifying

➢ Comparing and discussing alternatives

➢ Expressing opinions

➢ Explaining causes

➢ Unlikely/impossible conditions

➢ Agreeing/disagreeing

➢ Asking questions (2)

➢ Stating wishes and intentions/making plans

Example questions and possible answers for this test task:

Topic: accommodation

Function	Examples. (T: Teacher; S: Student)
Describing	T: Tell me about your house. What's your house like? What kind of house do you live in? S: I live in a new house near Ajlun. It has three bedrooms and a lounge.
Clarifying	T: I don't understand. Could you explain? Are those the only rooms in the house? No kitchen or bathroom? S: Of course, there's a kitchen and a bathroom, too. T: And a toilet? S: Yes, in the bathroom. T: Shower? S: No, we haven't got one.
Asking questions (1)	T: Now you ask me some questions. S: Where do you live? T: I live in a university apartment near the Language Center. S: Is it big? T: No, it's very small. S: Is it new? T: Yes, it is.

Exemplifying	T: What sort of things do you do in your home? Give me some examples of what you do at home. S: We eat and sleep. T: Is that all? S: No. T: What do you use the lounge for, for example? S: We sit and talk and watch TV.
Comparing and discussing alternatives	T: What's the difference between Ajlun and Irbid? S: Irbid's much bigger and uglier than Ajlun. T: Which is better? S: Ajlun. T: Why? S: It's in the country.
Expressing opinions	T: What do you think about the country? Do you think the country's good? S: I believe living in the country's good for children.
Explaining causes	T: What makes the country good for kids? S: It's cleaner. T: How does that help? S: They have fewer diseases.
Unlikely/impossible conditions	T: But, what if you had to live in a town? S: If I had to live in a big city, I would still be happy.
Agreeing/disagreeing	T: I don't think so. I wouldn't have thought so. You're wrong. Are you sure? You wouldn't, you know. S: Oh, yes, I would. Not as happy, but still happy.
Asking questions (2)	T: Now you ask me some more questions. S: Where would you like to live? T: Well, here is very convenient and I enjoy being able to walk to work. The Jordan Valley's very nice. S: Wouldn't you like to live in the country? Which is more important to you: convenience or fresh air? T: I don't have the choice.

Stating wishes and intentions/makin g plans	T: What will you do when you graduate? Where will you live in the future? S: I'll continue to live with my parents until I get married. Then I'll buy a house. T: How will you manage it? S: I will save hard and buy land.

(Example questions and possible answers for the other topics are omitted.)

Appendix 5 关于大学英语口语考试的调查问卷 (简短演讲、角色扮演、录音口试)

同学们：你们好！现就大学英语口语考试进行一次问卷调查. **请认真如实填写!** 您的意见不仅对我们的研究起着至关重要的作用, 而且将关系到广大学生的切身利益. 谢谢合作!

学校:　　　　　　**专业:**　　　　　　　　**姓名:**

1. 除了英语口试, 您的英语口语将来可能的应用方式为:
   A. 演讲　　B. 私人交谈　　C. 研讨会　　D. 贸易谈判　　　E.其它

2. 您是否赞成只有笔试成绩优秀的学生才有口试资格的规定?　A. 是　　　B. 否
   理由: _____

3. 以下两种口语考试形式，哪一种更能提供轻松的环境，让您能够更好地发挥口语水平?
   A. 三到四名考生面对两位考官的面试
   B. 考生各自对着机器录音, 然后由考官根据磁带评分的口试形式
   理由:_____

4. 口试前, 您是否希望考官大量提供有关话题的录音或文字资料?　A. 是　　B.否
   理由:_____

5. 以下两种口试题目类型, 您更喜欢哪一种?
   A. 就某个话题无目的地泛泛而谈
   B. 针对某一任务或问题,通过交谈去完成任务, 解决问题　　　　　　C.都不喜欢
   理由:_____

6. 您是否希望口试中给您提供一个模拟现实的情景, 而您在其中扮演一个特定的角色?
   A. 是　　　　　B. 否
   理由: _____

7. 在面试中, 您更希望和考生交谈还是和考官交谈?　　A. 考生　　　　B.考官
   理由: _____

8. 在面试中, 您更希望: A. 大家积极踊跃地提出问题, 阐述见解
   还是　B. 考生彼此互不联系地独自进行发言或讲述
   理由: _____

9. 口语考试时, 考生常用的策略有:
   A. 先打腹稿, 想好要点, 再根据要点发言
   B. 先讲开场白, 并说明主体分几部分讲, 约需多少时间等
   C. 几乎全部用英语思维, 直接以英语发言
   D. 几乎全部用汉语思维, 立即译成英语
   E. 使用同义词, 重复或解释等手段使人听懂
   F. 使用表情, 手势等使考官及同学明白自己的意思
   G. 不管考官和考生是否听懂, 只顾自己往下讲

H. 模仿其他考生的词汇, 句型结构等

I. 忽略听不懂的地方, 仅根据只字片语插话讨论

J. 遇到个别听不懂的地方时, 不打断对方, 猜对方大意, 以便让对话进行下去

K. 打断对方时, 说 "EXCUSE ME" 等; 请求重复时, 说 "PARDON" 等

a. 12 月 8 日晚的口试分为两部分:

在第一部分简短演讲(Mini-Speech) 中, 您用了上述策略中的＿＿＿＿＿＿＿＿＿＿＿

在第二部分角色扮演(Role Play)中, 您用了上述策略中的＿＿＿＿＿＿＿＿＿＿

b. 在直接面对机器录音的口试(Machine-recorded SET)中, 您用了上述策略中的

＿＿＿＿＿＿＿＿＿＿

10. 你在简短演讲(Mini-speech)的题目是什么? ＿＿＿＿＿＿＿＿＿＿＿＿

11. 你对三部分口试的总体评价如何? 它们的优缺点分别有哪些?

口试形式	总体评价	优点	缺点
简短演讲 (Mini-speech)	1. 很好 2. 较好 3. 一般 4. 较差 5. 很差		
角色扮演 (Role play)	a. 很好 b. 较好 c. 一般 d. 较差 e. 很差		
机器录音 (Machine-recorded SET)	a. 很好 b. 较好 c. 一般 d. 较差 e. 很差		

12. 在三种口试形式中, 你是否发挥出了你的最佳英语口语水平?

A. 在简短演讲中: 是 否 原因: ＿＿＿＿＿＿＿＿＿＿＿＿＿＿＿＿ 。

B. 在角色扮演中: 是 否 原因: ＿＿＿＿＿＿＿＿＿＿＿＿＿＿＿＿ 。

C. 在机器录音中: 是 否 原因: ＿＿＿＿＿＿＿＿＿＿＿＿＿＿＿＿ 。

Appendix 6 An SEAT test paper (Discussion and Presentation) (CHEN, 2000)

Name: _____   Number: _____

Section I. (12 minutes)

Directions: In this part, you will discuss the given topic in groups of four for about 10 minutes. Your performance will be evaluated according to your contribution to the discussion. In the discussion, take notes of what you think are important. Your notes will not be marked. But you may need the information later. You can take notes on this sheet. Don't get upset if the examiner interrupts you at the end of the time limit.

Section II. (10 minutes)

Directions: In this part, you will give an oral presentation on a given topic to four of your classmates for at least 5 minutes. After the presentation, you are going to answer any relevant questions from the audience.

Note-taking: You can take notes below. Your notes will not be marked. But it is important that you can understand them yourself. You may include some key words and phrases in your notes to remind you of the main ideas covered in the discussion session, but writing the complete sentences down is not allowed.

Test Item 1 Travel Planning

Task 1.1 Discussion: Travel planning –For Examinees

After staying in Zhijiang College for several months, you are homesick. You miss your family very much. Recently your class won the college basketball match and was awarded a prize. The head teacher has agreed to arrange a tour for the class. Isn't it a good opportunity to go home if the class agrees to take a trip to your hometown? But your classmates may have the same idea as you do. So you had better work out an attractive plan in terms of touring route, duration, touring expenses, etc. Now you can discuss your plan with the other three students and try to decide upon the best tour arrangement.

Remember that if you succeed in persuading others to accept your proposal, you are going to see your parents soon.

****

Task 1.2 Prestention: Travel Planning–For Examinees

You have just had a discussion with three classmates for around ten minutes. The class is waiting for the result of your discussion. You are going to give a presentation of around 5 minutes to them in which you can report the different ideas of the members and their reasons as well as the detailed travel plan you have worked out and after the report answer their questions. Now review your notes and organize your report mentally for about 2 minutes. Do not write anything from now on. Remember, during your report, you should be polite. At the beginning introduce yourself to the audience and in the end conclude your oral presentation and express your gratitude to them.

****

Task 1 Discussion: Travel Planning– For Audience

While you are waiting to be tested, you are not idle (闲的，无事可干的). Read the following situation and talk with the others around you. Your contribution to this discussion is not marked. But the examiner is observing your performance in this activity and it will affect your final score. Besides, it will help you understand the following report and each of you must ask the reporter some relevant questions afterwards.

Recently your class won the college basketball match and was awarded a prize. The head teacher has agreed to arrange a tour for the class. Four of your classmates have been asked to discuss about the tour arrangement. When they arrive at the final decision, one of them will give a report to you. Before the report, discuss with people around you and write down your expectations about the tour, such as low expenses. You may prepare a list of questions you are interested in about the tour, for example, is it far from Hangzhou? While listening to the report, see if you are satisfied with the arrangement and after it you can ask the reporter those questions in your list he/she has not covered in the report.

Test Item 2   A Problem Page

Task 2.1 Discussion: A Problem Page–for Examinees

The college has received such a letter from a parent in Nanjing, who is obviously having trouble in making up his (or her) mind.

Dear Sirs,

My daughter is now studying in a local key middle school. She will take the entrance examination next July. She is always a top student, so we are confident that she will pass it easily.

When she graduates from middle school, my daughter would like to go to Zhejiang University. But recently a friend has told us that all the first-year students are locked in Zhijiang College, a small campus far away from downtown. It is said that life there is hard and dull and students are cut off from the outside world. Is that the case? Why does the university adopt such a practice? How do students think of it? Are they enjoying themselves or are they suffering from inconveniences? I am deeply concerned because my daughter is used to city life and has never been far away from home yet.   I would appreciate it if you can provide me with opinions and experiences of some first-year students. Their attitudes to life in Zhijiang College may be of some help in our making the final decision.

Yours faithfully,

A worried parent

As requested, you are chosen to talk to the parent. Before the speech, you should talk with the others and decide upon what to tell the anxious father. After your report your audience may ask you several questions he/she is concerned about, so you must prepare fully. Try to be understanding and convincing.

Task 2.2 Presentation: A Problem Page–For Examinees

You have just had a discussion with three other first-year students for around ten minutes. The parent is now waiting in the meeting room. You are going to give a report of around 5 minutes to him/her and then answer his/her questions. Now review your notes and organize your report mentally for about 2 minutes. Do not write anything from now on. Remember, during your report, you should be polite. At the beginning introduce yourself to the audience and in the end conclude your oral presentation and express your gratitude to them.

Task 1   Discussion: A Problem Page–For Audience

While you are waiting to be tested, you are not idle (闲的，无事可干的). Read the following situation and talk with the others around you. Your contribution to this discussion is not marked. But the examiner is observing your performance in this activity and it will affect your final score. Besides, it will help you understand the following report and you must ask the reporter some questions afterwards.

Your daughter is now studying in a local key middle school. She will take the entrance examination next July. She is a top student, so you are sure that she will pass it easily. Therefore, your family are always discussing which university she should go after she graduates from middle school. Zhejiang University in Hangzhou is one of the choices. But recently a friend told you that all the first-year students are locked in Zhijiang

College, a small campus far away from downtown. It is said that life there is hard and dull and students are cut off from the outside world. You are not sure whether it is the case or not. You are deeply concerned because your daughter is used to convenient city life and has never been far away from home yet.

Now you are on a business trip to Hangzhou. The Students' Union will soon send a representative, a first-year student, to give a report on college life there. It is a good opportunity to know the college better because the information you get from the report will be valuable in your decision-making. Before he/she arrives, discuss with people around you and prepare a list of questions you would like to ask him/her. Later you may ask the reporter those questions he/she has not covered in the report or other relevant questions.

Test Item 3　　Donation

Task 3.1 Discussion: Donation(捐款)–For Examinees

Students' Union plays an important role in college life. The university has recently got a donation of 100,000 RMB from a local company. As members of the Students' Union, you are going to discuss what to do with the money and work out a proposal to the president. For some reason, the money can be used for **only one purpose**.

For your reference, here is the report of a recent survey done to all the first-year students in Zhejiang University.

> …28.7% of the students complain that most of the books in the library are too old and torn. They would like more up-to-date books. 25.9% of them think the computers in the university computer center are too old and slow and the university should purchase some new and advanced ones. 17.1% urge the university to improve the condition in the canteen and set up more supermarkets and stores. 10.9% suggest the university set up a foundation to help the poor students. 7.3% want their dormitories to be refurbished. 6.8%, mostly boys, propose a new football playground be built. 4.3% think an English Saloon is necessary…

Of course, you may also have your own ideas different from the above mentioned. Now discuss with other members and agree upon the final proposal.

****

Task 3.2 Presentation: Donation(捐款)–For Examinees

You have just had a discussion about how to make good use of a large sum of money to serve the students in this university with three classmates for around ten minutes. All the students and some important people in this university are waiting for the result of your discussion. You are going to give a presentation of around 5 minutes to them in which you can report the different ideas of the members and their reasons as well as the final agreement you have worked out and after the report answer any relevant questions from the audience. Now review your notes and organize your report mentally for about 2 minutes. Do not write anything from now on. Remember, during your report, you should be polite. At the beginning introduce yourself to the audience and in the end conclude your oral presentation and express your gratitude to them.

****

Task 3 Discussion: Donation(捐款)-For Audience

While you are waiting to be tested, you are not idle (闲的，无事可干的). Read the following situation and talk with the others around you. Your contribution to this discussion is not marked. But the examiner is observing your performance in this activity and it will affect your final score. Besides, it will help you understand the following report and you can ask the reporter some questions afterwards.

In a recent survey, students made a lot of suggestion to the university, such as buying more books for the library, buying some new computers. However, without money they can hardly be realized.

The university has recently got a donation of 100,000 RMB from a local company. Now members of the Students' Union are discussing what to do with the money and soon they will work out a proposal to the president. It is said that whatever use you make of the money, it can be spent for **one purpose only**.

What do you expect their proposal will be? Discuss with people around you before the representative from the Students' Union comes to give a report on their decision. Listen to him/her and see whether their proposal agrees with your expectation. After the report, each of you must ask the reporter at least one relevant question.

Test Item 4　　　Part-time Jobs

Task 4.1 Discussion: Part-time Jobs–For Examinees

Recently more and more first-year students in Zhijiang College are taking

142

on part-time jobs. The college administration therefore is greatly concerned about it. They want to know what impact it has on students' life and study. You and three other students are invited to introduce whatever you know about it, including your experiences or those of your friends. You are also expected to give your own opinions of the phenomenon and make suggestions to part-time job takers and college administration.

****

Task 4.2 Presentation: Part-time Jobs–For Examinees

You have just had a discussion about part-time jobs in universities and colleges for around ten minutes. All the students and some important people in this university are waiting for the result of your discussion. You are going to give a presentation of around 5 minutes to them in which you can report the different ideas of the members and their reasons as well as the final agreement you have worked out and after the report answer any relevant questions from the audience. Now review your notes and organize your report mentally for about 2 minutes. Do not write anything from now on. Remember, during your report, you should be polite. At the beginning introduce yourself to the audience and in the end conclude your oral presentation and express your gratitude to them.

****

Task 4 Discussion: Part-time Jobs–For Audience

While you are waiting to be tested, you are not idle (闲的，无事可干的). Read the following situation and talk with the others around you. Your contribution to this discussion is not marked. But the examiner is observing your performance in this activity and it will affect your final score. Besides, it will help you understand the following report and each of you must ask the reporter at least one question afterwards.

Recently more and more first-year students in Zhijiang College are taking on part-time jobs. The college administration therefore is greatly concerned about it. Four students have been invited to discuss about this phenomenon. Before the representative comes to give a report of the discussion, you may talk with people around you about the following questions.

Should first-year students take part-time jobs?

Why do they take part-time jobs?

What are the positive and negative effects of part-time jobs on students' life?

Is it possible for one to balance his study and part-time job?

…

Listen to the report attentively and see whether you can agree with the reporter. You can ask relevant questions after the presentation.

Test Item 5 Examination or Not?

Task 5.1 Discussion: Examination or Not?–For Examinees

After taking various examinations for so many years, you have become an experienced examination takers. How do you think of examinations? Are they doing more good to students than harm or more harm than good? You can speak of your own experiences. Can we do without examinations? If it were the case, how should teachers effectively evaluate students'' progress and without entrance examinations how should colleges and universities enroll new students? Discuss with other members in your group and work out your suggestions. If you think examinations are necessary, give your reasons and try to convince the others.

****

Task 5.2 Presentation: Examination or Not?–For Examinees

You have just had a discussion about whether examinations are necessary and without them how students should be assessed. In the office, the principals from some key universities and some well-known educators are waiting for your report. You should prepare a presentation of around 5 minutes in which you can include the process of your discussion, the different ideas of each member and their reasons as well as the final result. After the report, answer any relevant questions from the audience. Now review your notes and organize your report mentally for about 2 minutes. Do not write anything from now on. REMEMBER your audiences are VIPs (Very Important People) and you should be polite and respectful. So greet them and make a brief self-introduction to the audience and in the end conclude your oral presentation and express your gratitude to them.

****

Task 5 Discussion: Examinations or not-For Audience

While you are waiting to be tested, you are not idle (闲的，无事可干的). Read the following situation and talk with the others around you. Your contribution to this discussion is not marked. But the examiner is observing your performance in this activity and it will affect your final score. Besides, it will help you understand the following report and each of you must ask the reporter at least one question afterwards.

Some of you are principals of some top universities in China and some are famous educators. You have been aware that examination is not a perfect way of evaluating students'' achievement. Many students feel resentful and in a recent survey, the majority of the students admit that they have cheated in examinations for at least once. You think it may be necessary to reform the examination system. But you would like to know what are students'' opinions and in what way they would like to be tested. Shortly after, a representative will be sent to you to give a report. Before he/she arrives, discuss the topic with the other people around you and prepare some questions to ask the report later.

Test Item 6   A Mock Election

Task 6.1 Discussion: A Mock Election–For Examinees

In Zhijiang College, many students are eager to practice their English outside the classroom. But so far there are few organizations to help them improve it, especially spoken English. Now a group of English lovers are going to found an English club. You and three other students want to be the organizers and leaders in it. But many other candidates want the positions too. So you must run for it(参加竞选). Discuss with your partners and work out a detailed plan. Your plan should be competitive in terms of its name, location, size, activities and programs, facilities, fee and other aspects.

****

Task 6.2 Presentation: A Mock Election–For Examinees

You have just had a discussion about others about the English club. In the meeting room, the students, including other candidates, are waiting for you. You are going to give a running speech, in which you must state your plan clearly or they won't vote for you.   Your presentation should last for around 5 minutes. After the report, answer any relevant questions from the audience. Now review your notes and organize your report mentally for about 2 minutes. Do not write anything from now on. REMEMBER you must leave a good impression on your audience. So you should be polite and respectful. Stay calm. Greet your audience and make a brief self-introduction to them and in the end conclude your oral presentation and express your gratitude to them. Whether you can win the position is determined by your speech and the responses from the audience.

```
**************************************************
```

Task 6 Discussion: A Mock Election–For Audience

While you are waiting to be tested, you are not idle (闲的，无事可干的). Read the following situation and talk with the others around you. Your contribution to this discussion is not marked. But the examiner is observing your performance in this activity and it will affect your final score. Besides, it will help you understand the following report and each of you must ask the reporter at least one question afterwards.

In Zhijiang College, many students are eager to practice their English outside the classroom. But so far there are few organizations to help them improve it, especially spoken English. Recently, you hear a good piece of news–a group of English lovers are going to found an English club. Today some candidates are going to run for(竞选) the positions of leaders in the organization. Several minutes the first candidate will give a speech to you, in which he/she will state the general plan. Before he/she arrives, you can discuss with people around you. What kind of a person do you expect the future leader of the English club should be? What activities and programs will the club hold? What is its name? etc. You may have many other relevant questions. After the speech, you can ask the candidate the points he/she has not covered in the speech and decide if you are satisfied with the plan and whether you will vote for (投票选举)the candidate.

Test Item 7　　An Important Family Decision

Task 7.1 Discussion: An Important Family Decision–For Examinees

Recently more and more families are sending their children abroad. Parents think if one is sent abroad at an early age, he or she will adapt to （适应） the new environment quickly. Your neighbor has a distinct relative（远房亲戚） in the United States. And they are planning to send their 10-year-old daughter to stay with the relative and study in a local high school. Since you always regard the little girl as a younger sister, you think you are somehow responsible for their final decision. Therefore, you are going to have a discussion with some friends in the same neighborhood. You can remark on the popular phenomenon in society, give your own opinion and also listen to their opinions of your neighbor's plan. The parents have not made up their mind yet. Maybe they would like your advice later.

```
**************************************************
```

Task 7.2 Presentation: An Important Family Decision–For Examinees

You have just had a discussion with three friends in your neighborhood for around ten minutes. Now you are going to talk to your neighbor. You will give a presentation of around 5 minutes in which you can express and explain your own opinion as well as the opinions of your friends. Your advice may be very valuable for the family. After the presentation, answer any relevant questions from your audience. Now review your notes and organize your report mentally for about 2 minutes. Do not write anything from now on. Remember to knock at the door first before they answer.

****

Task 7 Discussion: An Important Family Decision–For Audience

While you are waiting to be tested, you are not idle (闲的，无事可干的). Read the following situation and talk with the others around you. Your contribution to this discussion is not marked. But the examiner is observing your performance in this activity and it will affect your final score. Besides, it will help you understand the following report and each of you must ask the reporter at least one question afterwards.

Recently more and more families are sending their children abroad. You know that a person can adapt to the new environment better if he is sent abroad at an early age. You have a distant relative in the United States, so you are planning to send your 10-year-old daughter to stay with them and study in a high school nearby. The decision will definitely influence the whole life of your daughter. So you are discussing it with the other family members, including your parents and parents-in-law. Shall you send the girl to a foreign country or shall you send her to a local school in your city? Is it good for a girl of 10 to live without parents around? Can she live a good life? What shall you prepare for her if you are determined to send her abroad? …Later someone is knocking at the door. Remember to ask who it is before you open the door. If the person comes to do you a favor, thank him/her sincerely.

Appendix 7 Presentation and discussion (P&D) as an SEAT format–Test specifications for the examiner

The presentation and discussion (P&D) is a spoken English test format designed for juniors and seniors. It is designed according to College English Syllabus (Revised edition) and is based on the cross-cultural thematic approach to the teaching and testing of spoken English.

Physical setting

Each round of P&D SET will be composed of three or four candidates and one examiner. The examiner gives brief instructions, controls the procedure and scores the candidates. They will be seated around a table (ideally a long one) as follows.

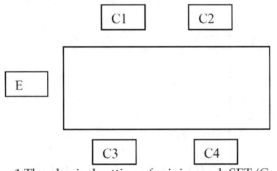

Figure 1 The physical setting of mini-speech SET (C: candidate, E: examiner)

Test content

The test includes two major tasks for each candidate. One is presentation and the other is discussion.

Preparation: (10 minutes)

Before the candidates perform the two tasks, each of them is presented the test paper, which includes a passage of between 350 to 400 words together with a topic for their presentation, and a sheet of paper for them to take notes. They are given 10 minutes to read the passage and prepare for the first task. They can use dictionaries, take notes and draft outlines for the presentation, but they are not allowed to communicate with each other, nor are they allowed to write on the test papers since other candidates will use them. In the end of the test, both the test papers and the notes will be handed in.

Test tasks: (10 minutes)

Task 1 Presentation (6 minutes)

The presentation is given within 1.5 minutes and should include at least three parts.

4) **Introduction:** This may include greetings, self-introduction, introduction of the topic to arouse the interest of the audience, presentation of key words and new vocabulary, etc.

5) **Main body:** This part is further divided into two sub-sections. One is called "summary", in which the candidate summarizes the passage guided by the question given. The other is called "relationship", in which the candidate relates what he/she reads to his/her life or ideas by answering the question given.

6) **Conclusion:** Here, the speaker will summarize his speech in a powerful, impressive, or inspirational way.

Part 2 Discussion (4 minutes)

This task is performed by the candidates according to a question given by the examiner.

Of course, in the end the speaker has to end the seminar in an appropriate way by announcing the end and by expressing gratitude to the audience.

Procedure

The procedure will be done according to the following flow chart.

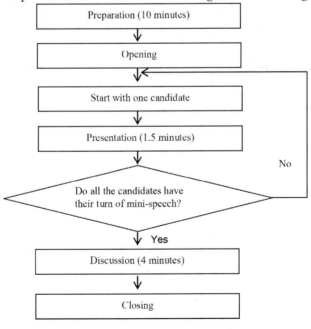

Figure 2: The procedural flow chart of mini-speech SET format

Topics

In the mini-speech, candidates choose what to talk about. The topic chosen has to be of general interest, controversial, centered around students' study and social lives and comprehensible without special technical knowledge. The speech and be narrative, argumentative, descriptive, expository or a combination of different styles. Cross-cultural topics are preferred for the simple reason of the only possible future needs of spoken English by the students to communicate in a cross-cultural situation. To summarize, the topic chosen has to follow the following guideline:

✓ **Of general interest**
✓ **Controversial**
✓ **Centered around students' lives**
✓ **Comprehensible without special knowledge**
✓ **Narrative, argumentative, descriptive, expository or a combination of the above**
✓ **Cross-cultural preferred.**

One warning is that if the candidates plagiarize other people's speeches, their scores will be reduced by half.

Topics

The topics provided by the candidates are broadly grouped into nine categories on the basis of a "key-word analysis". They are presented as follows.

Table 1 Topics selected by candidates in the mini-speech SET

Type	Sub-type	Number	Total
College study	Methodology	1	5
	Examination system	2	
	English learning	1	
	Plagiarism	1	
Entertainment	Hobby and interest	2	3
	Music and Movie	1	
Sports	Basketball	2	4
	Football	1	
	Famous athletes	1	
Background	Family	1	3
	Hometown	1	
	City life and country life	1	

Science and technology	Internet	2	5
	Software	1	
	Creation and invention	1	
	Uses of salt	1	
Fashions	Private cars	1	4
	Part-time jobs	3	
Human relationship	Children and parents	1	3
	Man-woman relationship	2	
Personality	Traits leading to success	1	2
	Independence	1	
Others	Fresh water	1	7
	Festival-Christmas	1	
	How to keep healthy	1	
	Famous people	1	
	Opening-up and reform	1	
	Patriotism	1	
	War and peace	1	
Sum			36

Criteria for assessment (Speech and seminar)

The criteria for assessment will be applied not only to the speeches given, but also to the questions and answers between the speaker and the audience.

- ✓ **Content (Components of the speech complete, main ideas standing out and details substantive)**
- ✓ **Accuracy (Correct use of pronunciation, vocabulary and structure)**
- ✓ **Range (A wide range of vocabulary and structure)**
- ✓ **Fluency (Appropriate speed, stress and intonation)**
- ✓ **Discourse management (Cohesion and coherence)**
- ✓ **Register or appropriacy (Use of language appropriate to context, function and intention)**
- ✓ **Strategy (Effective use of linguistic and non-linguistic strategies)**
- ✓ **Participation (The audience's ability to ask questions and to present one's own ideas on the speeches during each seminar session)**

Score description

Table 3 Score description

90-100	Excellent

80-89.5	Good
70-79.5	Average
60-69.5	Acceptable
Below 60	Poor or failure

Rating scale

In formulating the rating scale, I have classified the assessment criteria into four groups and give them equal weighting. I have also combined the system of degree of skills with the 100-point marking system, the latter being already traditionally accepted. However, a different weighting of the above mentioned assessment criteria can be used according to different testing situations.

Another decision has to be made about rating is whether a holistic or analytic approach should be adopted. In the former CET-SET practice, the combination of both is employed. In our experiment, we used both and the examiner gives a holistic score based on the analytic rating scale given.

Table 2 Rating scales

Scores	Content	Language		Meta-language
	Content	Accuracy and range	Fluency and discourse management	Register, strategy and participation
22.5-25 Excellent	➢ Components of the speech complete ➢ Main ideas standing out ➢ Details substantive	➢ Correct pronunciation ➢ Correct use of vocabulary and structure ➢ A wide range of vocabulary and structure	➢ Appropriate speed, stress and intonation ➢ Effective use of cohesive devices ➢ Coherence achieved	➢ Use of language appropriate to context, function and intention ➢ Effective use of linguistic and non-linguistic strategies ➢ The audience's ability to ask questions and to present one's own ideas during discussion session
20-22.5 Good	➢ Lack of necessary components in the subsections of the speech ➢ Main ideas clear but not very powerful ➢ Details stated but not enough	➢ Containing a little pronunciation errors ➢ Containing a little errors in vocabulary and structure ➢ A basically satisfactory range of vocabulary and structure to deal with the topic	➢ Speed a little hasty or slow, a little wrong stress and intonation ➢ Adequate use of cohesive devices ➢ Satisfactory logic and coherence	➢ Occasionally containing language too formal or too casual ➢ Satisfactory use of linguistic and non-linguistic strategies ➢ Having some difficulty to ask questions and to present one's ideas
17.5-20 Average	➢ Lack of necessary components in the subsections of the speech ➢ Main ideas stated but not very powerful ➢ Details stated	➢ Containing pronunciation errors not affecting communication ➢ Containing grammatical errors not affecting communication ➢ Adequate range of vocabulary to convey ideas	➢ Prolonged silence or some wrong stress and intonation ➢ Containing use of cohesive devices ➢ Acceptable logic and coherence	➢ Containing some language too formal or too casual. ➢ Some linguistic and non-linguistic strategies used ➢ Able to ask questions and present one's own ideas
15-17.5 Acceptable	➢ Lack a major subsection in the speech ➢ Main ideas not clear ➢ Some details irrelevant	➢ Errors of pronunciation affect communication ➢ Errors of vocabulary and communication affecting communication ➢ A minimum range of vocabulary and structure	➢ Inappropriate speed, wrong stress and intonation affecting communication ➢ Occasional or wrong use of cohesive devices ➢ Cohesion not well achieved	➢ Register of language affecting communication ➢ Occasional or some wrong use of strategies ➢ Not able to ask questions or ideas irrelevant
Below 15 Poor or failure	➢ Subsections not obvious ➢ Main ideas not stated ➢ Most details irrelevant or no supporting details	➢ Full of errors on pronunciation ➢ Full of errors on vocabulary and structure ➢ Vocabulary and structure scarce and repetitive	➢ Inability to control speed, full of stress and intonation errors ➢ No use of cohesive devices ➢ Coherence very bad	➢ Register of language cause inability of communication ➢ No or totally wrong use of strategies ➢ Unable to present questions and one's own ideas

Appendix 8 考生须知(发言与讨论)

一、考试简介

1. 考试性质与对象

发言与讨论(Presentation and Discussion 简称 P&D)根据《大学英语教学大纲(修订本)》用于测量我国非英语专业大学生基础阶段第三、四级英语口语交际能力。

2. 考试形式

P&D 考试采取面试形式，每场考试由 1 名考官和 4 名(或 3 名)考生组成。交际活动主要在考生之间展开，考官负责过程的实施和打分。

3. 试题构成

考生在口试前，从考官处领取试题和便条，然后准备 10 分钟。试题包括一篇 350-400 单词的文章和对考生发言的要求。正式考试包括两项任务。

任务	时间	题型	说明
Task 1	8 分钟	发言	每位考生围绕概述 (Summary) 和联系 (Relationship)两个分话题进行发言，即根据试卷提示首先概述阅读文章内容，然后联系自己思想和生活实际发言。整个发言应当包括引子(Introduction)、主体(Main body)和结语(Conclusion)三个部分。每位考生发言不得超过 2 分钟。
Task 2	7 分钟	讨论	考生根据考官口头提出的问题进行讨论。

4. 话题范围

P&D 考试选取能引起考生兴趣，与考生过去、现在或将来生活有关的有争议性的话题。

5. 评分标准

评分标准分为内容、语言和元语言三大块，涉及发言完整性、语言准确性、词汇结构多样性、语言流利性、语篇连贯性、语言适切性、交际策略使用和交际参与意识等8项指标。

6. 等级描述

评分采用百分制和等级描述相结合的方法，以尊重传统习惯和分数转换的方便。

等级	百分制	描述
A.优秀	90-100	发言内容完整；语言准确、富于变化、流畅自然，没有语言错误；善于运用交际策略，讨论中有很好的参与意识。
B.良好	80-89	发言内容基本完整；语言比较准确、多样、流畅，有少许语言错误，但不影响交际；比较善于运用交际策略，讨论中有较好的参与意识。

C.中等	70-79	发言内容部分欠缺；语言基本准确、多样、流畅，有少量语言错误，但能够达意；能够运用交际策略，讨论中有一定参与意识。
D.及格	60-69	发言内容欠缺某些主要部分；语言基本准确、多样、流畅，有少量语言错误，并影响交际；偶尔运用交际策略，讨论中参与意识不强。
E. 不及格	60 以下	发言内容严重欠缺，有些发言与话题无关；语言错误百出、词汇结构重复单一、不时有停顿，表达意义不连贯，严重影响交际；不能或错误地运用交际策略，讨论中参与意识差。

二、注意事项

1. 考生应携带笔、身份证或学生证(可以带一本词典)在候考室等候参加考试，在候考期间不得随意离开候考室。经考官指定的班干部许可后，方可到指定的卫生间。

2. 考生应按照事先分好的小组，在班干部的允许下提前几分种到达考场；

3. 正式考试前考生应当独立准备发言。可以在发给的便条上作笔记，列提纲，但不得在考卷上写划，不得互相传阅考卷，不得进行交谈；发言前要将考卷交给考官；

4. 每位考生发言部分时间不得超过 2 分钟，因此应当认真计划，在规定时间内完成发言各部分内容。届时如果还未讲完，考官将打断考生发言。发言内容不全将影响口试成绩；

5. 在讨论部分，考生对话应简明扼要。如果讲话时间过长，考官有权打断其讲话；

6. 考试结束后，考生须上交便条，之后必须立即离开考区。

Appendix 9 A set of test papers for the P&D SEAT

Passage 1 How do people celebrate the Spring Festival?

The Spring Festival is celebrated at the turn of a Chinese calendar year. It starts on the Eve of the Lunar New Year, the last night of the old year. Its length varies from place to place. However, most parts of the country celebrate it for four days, until the third of the first month.

On New Year's Eve, each family has its members gathered together and eats a family reunion dinner. From that, you can really feel what the Chinese call "chi wenhua", or "the culture of eating". Everything is amazing and delicious. The result is that though your stomach has been fully filled with the food, you still take up your chopsticks.

After the meal everyone will watch TV until the clock strikes twelve. Immediately, the deafening sound of firecrackers, with which people greet the arrival of the New Year, can be heard everywhere. Because of some safety reasons, all cities don't allow firecrackers, while in the country, people can still use this way to welcome the New Year.

In the Western countries, it is traditional for one to be with one's family on Christmas Day. They think it is family time. But in China, it is sort of the custom that once one has had his meal, he goes off to spend some time with other friends or other family and greet each other with the best wishes. "Happy New Year!" is the usual greeting you would hear them say to each other.

Unfortunately, the Spring Festival is changing in the way that traditional festival, like Thanksgiving and Christmas, also changes in the US. In America, Christmas has long become a very commercialized thing. It becomes less of a just happy giving time, but more of a time that you just have to go out a lot and buy gifts for your friends. And that may be slowly happening to Chinese too. People begin to have a little more money. Since the airplane and bus travel is getting more common, people are more mobile. So maybe they see their family several times a year. They talk to them on the phone. They even have email now. It is less of a time that a family can really come back together. It makes the SPECIALNESS of the Spring Festival go away a little bit. (386 words)

Topic of your presentation: **How do people celebrate the Spring Festival: customs and changes?**

Your presentation should be **focused on the following two sections:**

✓ **Summary:** How do people usually celebrate the Spring Festival?

✓ **Relationship:** What changes are occurring concerning the Spring Festival and Christmas? What do you think the reasons are for the changes?

Attention: Your presentation should be **no longer than 2 minutes**. The examiner will stop you if you exceed the time limit!

Passage 2 My Spring Festival

My name is Li Ming. I am a college student. Now that the Spring Festival is over, I am look forward to going back to college. It's really funny, I find myself more and more eager to be back to the campus life.

As usual I can get little work done during the winter vacation. For one thing, the Spring Festival is always a big distraction, and for days before and after nobody can get any work done. It's all right if you really have a nice time, as I used to. But now I find myself enjoying it less and less. I stopped enjoying fireworks and firecrackers years ago. The firecrackers especially get on my nerves. I really think we should stop making them, as every year many children have their eyes hurt or even blinded. Even worse sometimes fires are started and whole buildings get burned down. Still I suppose some people will continue to make them as long as there is a market for them.

And the food! People spend days queuing and buying. The result – too much food which does nobody any good. Chicken, duck, fish, pork, beef, mutton, – name whatever you want, you have it. What's more, they become tasteless too. Too much of a good thing, as we say, makes it bad. And this visiting business too! It's all right for a few really good friends to get together and chat over some tea or drinks. But mere acquaintances and the usually not too neighborly neighbors dropping in to say hello – well, I suppose these are well-intended gestures, but I find them a pain in the neck. Usually there is nothing to talk about except some meaningless platitudes.

Mum is looking very tired, and no wonder Dad too, I think, found the whole thing a stain. The only two who seemed to enjoy the Spring Festival are Granny and my younger brother Xiao Hong.

Oh yes, I did enjoy myself skating on the nearby lake quite a few times. I stopped going before the Spring Festival because the ice is getting very thin. But there are people who are either too reckless or too ignorant or both, and we hear about people falling through the thin ice every year.

(368 words)

Topic of your presentation: **Experiences of the Spring Festivals: likes and dislikes**

Your presentation should be focused on the following two sections:

✓ Summary: Did Li Ming enjoy his last Spring Festival? Why or why not?

✓ Relationship: Which part of the Spring Festival do you like? Which part do you dislike? Give brief reasons.

Attention: Your presentation should be **no longer than 2 minutes**. The examiner will stop you if you exceed the time limit!

Passage 3 Santa Claus brings joy at Christmas

In many countries of the world, the celebration of Christmas on December 25th is a high point of the year. Santa Claus–also known as Saint Nicholas, has become a symbol of this festival. Pictures will be seen everywhere of the old man with long white beard, red coat, and bag of toys. Children are taught that he brings them presents the night before Christmas, and many children really believe this is true. In most countries, it is said that he lives near the North Pole, and arrives through the sky on a sledge sleigh (snow-cart) pulled by reindeer (驯鹿). He comes into houses down the chimney at midnight and places presents for the children in socks or bags by their beds or in front of the family Christmas tree. In shops or at children's parties, someone will dress up as Father Christmas and give small presents to children, or ask them what gifts they want for Christmas.

There are many stories and legends of his miracles and goodness. One of the most famous is the story of the three unmarried daughters of a once-wealthy man who could not afford to pay a dowry (嫁妆) for his daughters, and therefore they could not marry. In those days, a father had to give a lot of dowries to the prospective husband in order for a marriage to take place. Because he had no money, he was going to have to sell his daughters into slavery. Saint Nicholas overheard the weeping and crying of the father and daughters while walking past their house. Although he did not have much money left by that time, he had enough left for three bags of gold. The first bag of gold he secretly threw through the window in the night, and soon after, the girl was married.

When the second daughter came of age, a second bag of gold was also thrown through the window, in secret. When the third daughter came of age, Saint Nicholas threw it down the chimney, and it landed in a stocking that had been placed by the fireplace to dry. This night, the father hid himself in the dark and discovered that Saint Nicholas was the generous helper. That's why children hang their stockings beside their bed or the chimney on the Christmas Eve. (387 words)

Topic of your presentation: **Santa Claus comes to China**

Your presentation should be focused on the following two sections:

✓ Summary: Summarize the story about Santa Claus and the three unmarried girls.

✓ Relationship: Why are so many people in China celebrating Christmas?

Attention: Your presentation should be **no longer than 2 minutes**. The examiner will stop you if you exceed the time limit!

Passage 4 A Legend of Qingming Festival (Pure Brightness Day)

Qingming Festival (Pure Brightness Day) is also called Hanshi (cold food) Festival or Tomb-sweeping Day (Apr. 5 of the Lunar Calendar). A legend about the origin of the festival happened in the Spring and Autumn (Warring States) period. Zhong Er(重耳) was the eldest prince of the State of Jin (晋国) and was supposed to be the king after his father's death. But his younger brother wanted to murder him to succeed to the throne. One of the ministers, Jie Zitui(介子推), heard of the plot and helped the prince to escape successfully.

One day, they got lost in a great mountain and had nothing to eat for several days. The prince almost starved to death. He sat on the ground and exclaimed, "Oh, Good Heavens! It's nothing for me to die, but I'm afraid my people will suffer." On hearing this, Jie went away to a quiet place and cut off a piece of flesh from his own leg. He roasted the flesh on fire and gave it to the prince. The prince ate it right away. When the prince was told that it was Jie's flesh, he was deeply moved and promised to reward the devoted minister. Yet Jie told him that his sole wish was to see him become a wise king and administer the State well.

Nineteen years later, Zhong at last returned and became the king of the State of Jin. He offered high posts and other favors to all who followed and helped him during the exile (流放生涯) but could not find Jie. It turned out that Jie, together with his old mother, had gone to a mountain covered with trees. Zhong ordered his men to search for him in the mountain but in vain. Someone suggested that he set a fire in the forest to force Jie to come out. This he did, but Jie didn't show up. He was finally found dead,

159

leaning against a tree with his old mother on his back. The king was extremely sad and regretful. In order to memorialize his lifesaver, he gave an order that from then on no one should cook with fire on that day. Even today, some families in the countryside still keep the custom. They bake hard bread and boil eggs the night before. They eat cold food for the whole day. (392 words)

Topic of your presentation: **A Legend of Qingming Festival**

Your presentation should be focused on the following two sections:

- Summary: Summarize the story about the origin of Hanshi Festival.

- Relationship: Briefly comment on Jie Zitui's behavior

Attention: Your presentation should be **no longer than 2 minutes**. The examiner will stop you if you exceed the time limit!

Topic for the oral discussion: Western festivals coming to China: a bless or a curse?
It seems that young people today are gradually losing interest in some traditional Chinese festivals. Instead, many of them begin to celebrate western festivals such as Christmas, Valentine's Day and Halloween. Do you think it good or bad? Give your reasons.

Appendix 10 Presentation and Discussion (P&D) Spoken English Test

Examiners' Material
Topic: Festivals

Preparation (10 minutes)

Examiner: Good morning /Good afternoon, everybody. Now I will give you the test paper and the note sheet. You have ten minutes to prepare for your presentation. You can use your dictionary, write on the note sheet, but you should not write or mark on the test paper. Are you clear?

Task 1 Presentation (8 minutes)

Examiner: Now come in and sit down. (when everyone takes his/her seat)Would you please write down your name and admission number on my rating sheet? (pointing at the right place on the rating sheet)Ok, right here. ... Now, please give me your test papers.

(when the test papers are collected)OK. Today, we will talk about festivals. Now, you can begin your presentation. Mr. /Miss. X, would you start first, please? (if the presentation exceeds the time limit) Excuse me, Mr. /Miss. X, your time is over. (when the first candidate finishes his/her presentation) Have you finished Mr. /Miss. X? (pointing at the second candidate) It's your turn. Mr. /Miss. X....

Task 2 Discussion (7 minutes)

(when everyone finishes the presentation) Now let's move on to the second task, the discussion topic for the oral discussion is "Western festivals coming to China: a bless or a curse?"

It seems that young people today are gradually losing interest in some traditional Chinese festivals. Instead, many of them begin to celebrate western festivals such as Christmas, Valentine's Day and Halloween. Do you think it good or bad? Give your reasons.

(when no one responds, the examiner may point at a certain candidate, preferably one who did well in the presentation) Mr. /Miss. X, why don't you break the ice first?

(when someone is dominating the discussion and keeps talking for over 1.5 minutes) Excuse me, Mr. /Miss. X, I am afraid you've been talking too long. Why don't we listen to what other people would say?

(if one candidate remains silence) Mr. /Miss. X, you seem to have been thinking for quite a long time. You must have something interesting to tell us about the issue.

(when time is up) Well, everybody, time is up, and that's the end of the test. Thank you. You may leave now.

Appendix 11 大学英语期末口语考试问卷调查 (发言与讨论)

同学们：你们好！现就大学英语期末口试进行一次问卷调查，**请认真如实填写**！你的意见对我们改进大学英语口语考试及教学将起到宝贵的参考作用。谢谢合作!

班级：_____ 姓名：_____ 学号：_____

第一部分：基本情况

1. 你认为自己的口语水平在班上同学中大约位于哪个等级？A. 优秀 B. 良好 C. 中等 D. 较差 E. 很差

2. 你认为是否有必要在期末英语考试中包括口语考试？

A. 是 理由：	B. 否 理由：
1) 口语是英语中不可缺少的一项技能； 2) 能够促进平日进行口语练习； 3) 笔试与口试成绩不一定成正比，笔试成绩好不见得口语就一定好； 4) 对外交流不断增多，口语日益重要； 5) 自己希望了解一下自己的口语水平和进步情况； 6) 其他(请具体说明)	1) 笔试成绩能够代表口语水平； 2) 应当减少考试，以减轻学生压力； 3) 学生读、听、写、译能力还未过关，目前进行口试还为时尚早； 4) 其他(请具体说明)

3. 以下两种口语考试形式，哪一种更能提供轻松的环境，让你能够更好地发挥口语水平？

A. 面试　　　　理由：	B. 机器录音　　　理由：
1) 机器情感和表情，面对机器没有交流的气氛和愿望； 2) 面对机器容易心理紧张，与人打交道比较放松； 3) 面试与实际口语交际较为接近，有利于今后应用； 4) 面试时听不懂还可以当场询问，而机器录音时不能与人进行多回合的双向交流，没有根据反馈进行修正的可能； 5) 其他(请具体说明)	1) 面试怕当场让人看出语言弱点，容易紧张； 2) 面试中若考官或考生发音不准，无法听懂，影响交流；机器录音不存在这个问题； 3) 录音评分没有印象分，较为客观； 4) 其他(请具体说明)

4. 在面试中, 你更希望和考生交谈还是和直接与考官交谈?

A. 考生　　　　理由：	B. 考官　　　　理由：
1) 考生之间较为平等，没有压力；面对考官则有一定心理恐惧； 2) 考生之间有较为相似的年龄和社会经验，能够有共同语言； 3) 考生之间可以互相鼓励，互相提醒，互相竞争； 4) 其他(请具体说明)	1) 面试中若考生发音不准，无法听懂，影响交流；考官一般口语较好，不存在这个问题； 2) 其他(请具体说明)

5. 口试前, 你是否希望考官提供与话题有关的文字资料?

A. 是　　　　　理由：	B. 否　　　　　理由：
1) 有利于考生进行内容和语言的准备，不至于无话可说； 2) 其他(请具体说明)	1) 没有资料更有利于自由发挥； 2) 其他(请具体说明)

第二部分：对本次口试看法

本次口试连续考两场，第一场是根据阅读文章发言并讨论，第二场是先热身，再根据图片发言和讨论，最后回答考官问题。

1.下列这些陈述多大程度上符合你的实际做法(而不是想法)？

　　　1＝完全不适合　2＝基本不适合　3＝部分适合　4＝基本适合　5＝完全适合

关于策略的陈述	第一场符合情况	第二场符合情况
A. 准备时在便条上写好完整句子或段落，发言时背诵	1　2　3　4　5	1　2　3　4　5
B. 准备时做笔记，列提纲或要点，再根据要点发言	1　2　3　4　5	1　2　3　4　5
C. 先讲开场白，并说明主体分几部分讲，最后有结束语	1　2　3　4　5	1　2　3　4　5
D. 上来就说，没有一定的次序，讲得越多越好，直到考官打断自己为止	1　2　3　4　5	1　2　3　4　5
E. 几乎全部用英语思维，直接以英语发言	1　2　3　4　5	1　2　3　4　5
F. 几乎全部用汉语思维，立即译成英语	1　2　3　4　5	1　2　3　4　5
G. 使用同义词，重复或解释等手段使他人听懂	1　2　3　4　5	1　2　3　4　5
H. 使用表情，手势等使考官及同学明白自己的意思	1　2　3　4　5	1　2　3　4　5
I. 不管考官和考生是否听懂，只顾自己往下讲	1　2　3　4　5	1　2　3　4　5
J. 模仿其他考生的词汇，句型结构等	1　2　3　4　5	1　2　3　4　5
K. 他人发言时，我忽略所有听不懂的部分，仅根据只字片语	1　2　3　4　5	1　2　3　4　5

插话讨论		
L. 遇到个别听不懂的地方时，不打断对方，猜对方大意，以便让对话进行下去	1　2　3　4　5	1　2　3　4　5
M. 打断对方时，说"EXCUSE ME"等；请求重复时，说"PARDON"等	1　2　3　4　5	1　2　3　4　5

2. 在两场口试中，你是否发挥出了你的口语水平？

第一场	1. 发挥极差　2. 发挥较差　3. 发挥一般　4. 发挥较好　5. 发挥很好
第二场	1. 发挥极差　2. 发挥较差　3. 发挥一般　4. 发挥较好　5. 发挥很好

3. 第二场口试所提供的文字材料在一下几个方面是否合适？

1. 话题是否令人感兴趣？	A．是　B．否
2. 语汇是否熟悉？	A．是　B．否
3. 难度是否适中？	A．是　B．偏难　C．偏易
4. 长度是否合适？	A．是　B．偏长　C．偏短

4. 你对两场口试的总体评价如何？它们的优缺点分别有哪些？需要如何改进？

场次	总体评价	优点	缺点	改进意见
第一场	1. 很差 2. 较差 3. 一般 4. 较好 5. 很好			
第二场	1. 很差 2. 较差 3. 一般 4. 较好 5. 很好